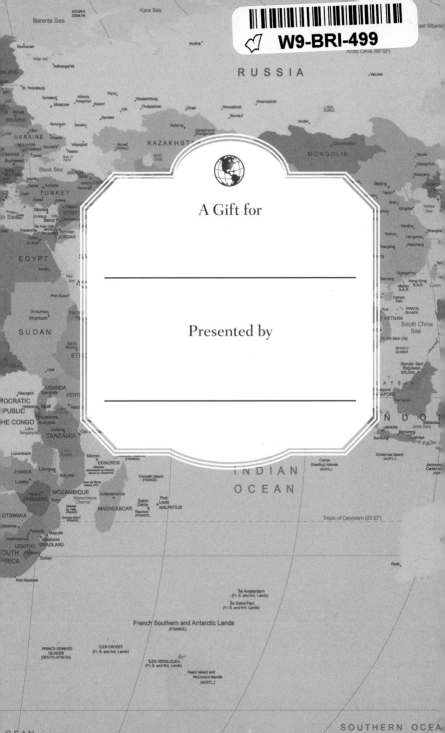

A Gift for

_____

Presented by

_____

I Used to Know That

GEOGRAPHY

"Without geography, you're nowhere."

—JIMMY BUFFETT

I Used to Know That

GEOGRAPHY

stuff you forgot
from school

WILL WILLIAMS
CAROLINE TAGGART

Reader's
Digest

The Reader's Digest Association, Inc.
New York, NY / Montreal

A READER'S DIGEST BOOK

Copyright © 2011 Michael O'Mara Books Limited

All rights reserved. Unauthorized reproduction, in any manner, is prohibited.

Reader's Digest is a registered trademark of The Reader's Digest Association, Inc.

First published in Great Britain by Michael O'Mara Books Limited, 9 Lion Yard, Tremadoc Road, London SW4 7NQ

READER'S DIGEST TRADE PUBLISHING

U.S. Project Editor: Andrea Chesman
Copy Editor: Barbara Booth
Project Production Coordinator: Rich Kershner
Senior Art Director: George McKeon
Executive Editor, Trade Publishing: Dolores York
Manufacturing Manager: Elizabeth Dinda
Associate Publisher, Trade Publishing: Rosanne McManus
President and Publisher, Trade Publishing: Harold Clarke

Library of Congress Cataloging in Publication Data
is available upon request
ISBN 13: 978-1-60652-245-5

Reader's Digest is committed to both the quality of our products and the service we provide to our customers. We value your comments, so please feel free to contact us:
The Reader's Digest Association, Inc., Adult Trade Publishing, 44 S. Broadway, White Plains, NY, 10601

For more Reader's Digest products and information, visit our website:

www.rd.com (in the United States)
www.readersdigest.ca (in Canada)

Printed in the United States of America

1 3 5 7 9 10 8 6 4 2

CONTENTS

Preface

The teaching of geography has changed beyond recognition over the last few decades. I was a member of what my coauthor Will Williams calls the "capes and bays" generation: We learned the names of places and the heights of mountains, but it never crossed anyone's mind to take us outside to stroll along a beach or wade through a river so we could see for ourselves how these things actually worked. And certainly no one ever tried to persuade me into believing that geography was fascinating because it was all around me, an unavoidable and ever-changing part of my daily life—and the daily life of everyone else in the world.

When Will and I set out to write this book, our primary goal was to bring the subject alive by demonstrating two things: (1) just how relevant geography is to each one of us and (2) just how wide ranging it is, encompassing science, economics, and sociology, not to mention the geographical sub-disciplines of geology, geomorphology, tectonics, and others too numerous to mention. Even if you are young enough to have been taught the theory of how landscapes changed over time or the economic and social importance of population growth, you are sure to find new insights in this book. If you are one of those who never got any further than memorizing the names of the world's major rivers, you will find surprises galore.

In other words, whether this book becomes for you a trip down memory lane, a voyage of discovery, or a companion for future crossword puzzle clues, *I Used to Know That: Geography* has something to offer anyone with an interest in the workings of this planet and the people who live on it. And if that sounds like a sweeping claim—well, that's geography for you.

—Caroline Taggart

Introduction

We have the ancient Greek scholar Ptolemy to thank for the study of geography. In the second century A.D. he wrote the very first book on the subject, fittingly called *Geographia*. His massive work offered instruction on laying out maps, provided coordinates for about 8,000 places, and discussed latitude and longitude. His book quickly became a best seller and was extremely influential. By the 1400s his work was translated into Latin, and travelers, scholars, and explorers, such as Christopher Columbus, came to depend on it.

Ptolemy defined his subject as "a representation of the whole known world together with the phenomena which are contained therein." The whole known world, then, is the scope of geography—and we know a lot more about planet Earth than Ptolemy did back in his day! Although geography can be taught as a separate subject, most of us learned about geography as part of our history, social studies, and Earth science classes. It fit into such diverse subjects because the study of geography encompasses both *physical* geography (why some of the world is forest and some desert, why volcanoes erupt) and *human* geography (why people live where they do and the way they do).

Another way to study geography is to divide the world up into pieces—oceans and continents—and start from there, which is what this book does. Along the way, we'll learn how the distance we are from the equator affects our climate (meteorology), why earthquakes occur (plate tectonics), and how one fish—the cod—changed North America (history). We'll consider population growth (arguably biology, possibly sociology) and its impact on the world and its resources (economics).

There is almost nothing that geography doesn't rub up against, and that is why it is so important. It seeks to understand the Earth and all of its human and natural intricacies—not only where objects are, but how they have changed and come to be.

Take the debate over climate change. Be it environmental concerns about the impact of fossil-fuel combustion, economic concerns over food supply, scarcity concerns about fresh water, or political concerns over one country's influence on another—it simply doesn't matter. Geographers are the ones who can bring together the disparate fields of inquiry to provide the ideas for moving to the next stage of development, for the simple reason that when geography spreads its wings, it embraces every aspect of the discussion.

Geography is a fluid, ever-changing, gigantic octopus of a subject, full of familiar terms and some less so. Read on to revisit what you used to know and catch up on some of the things you didn't.

Chapter 1

Welcome to Planet Earth

*Some 4.6 billion years ago our **sun** condensed out of a cloud of gas. That cosmic event left a lot of material behind—not exactly space rubbish, but plenty of dust and debris. Some of that debris eventually came together to form the **Earth** and the other **planets**. It wasn't a very tidy process, which is why we have lots of meteors (falling stars, or leftover material) dashing across the sky from time to time.*

HERE'S LOOKING AT YOU

There are lots of ways to look at the Earth and describe its features. Let's start with some of the basics, courtesy of the earliest mapmakers (cartographers) and geographers. Words in boldface throughout this book denote the first time you will come across these terms.

IMAGINARY LINES: LONGITUDE AND LATITUDE

Maps and globes are divided into lines of **longitude** (from North Pole to South Pole) and **latitude** (parallel to the equator), courtesy of Ptolemy, the world's first geographer. Longitude and latitude give us a reasonably easy, precise, and universal way of pinpointing any specific location on Earth, especially in the ocean, where landmarks are scarce.

If you drew an imaginary line on the Earth's surface equidistant from the North and South poles, this would be the **equator**. The line divides the Earth into a **Northern Hemisphere** and a **Southern Hemisphere** at the Earth's widest point. It is the point on Earth where the sun is directly overhead at noon on March 21, the **Spring Equinox**, and at noon on September 21, the **Fall Equinox.** Looking at a globe of the Earth, the first thing you notice is that most of the landmasses of the Earth are in the Northern Hemisphere, so all things aren't really equal.

There are two other imaginary lines running east to west around the globe: the **Tropic of Cancer** and the **Tropic of Capricorn**. The equator lies at 0 degrees latitude. The Tropic of Cancer is located at 23.5° north of the equator and is the spot on the planet where the sun is directly overhead at noon on June 21, the summer solstice in the Northern Hemisphere and the beginning of winter in the Southern Hemisphere. The Tropic of Capricorn lies at 23.5° south of the equator and is the spot where the sun is directly overhead at noon on December 21, the winter solstice in the Northern Hemisphere and the beginning of summer in the Southern Hemisphere.

WHY IS NORTH ALWAYS AT THE TOP OF MAPS?

In the early days of mapmaking, it wasn't. Often, Jerusalem, a holy site in the "East," was set at the top. But once globes became popular during the Renaissance, it seemed logical to put North on the top side for easy viewing of the "important" landmasses (Europe).

The equator, based on the sun's position, was an obvious place to call ground zero, or 0 degrees of latitude. But where on Earth to call 0 degrees of longitude? Mapmakers puzzled over this, and various solutions were proposed historically, mainly using a country's capital as 0 degrees for maps made in that country. But in 1884, when Great Britain ruled the waves, so to speak, the International Meridian Conference adopted the Greenwich meridian as the universal **prime meridian**, or zero point of longitude. The Greenwich meridian runs though the Royal Observatory in England.

GEO GEM

Blue Planet
We've always known that Mars was the Red Planet, because that's how it looks to us. It wasn't until astronauts left the Earth that they were able to look back and see that ours is a "Blue Planet." Earth appears to be blue because about 70 percent of the surface is covered by water.

CLIMATE ZONES

The world is divided up into zones based on latitude, and knowing these makes understanding climate a little easier. Starting at the "top" of the globe, these are:

- Arctic Circle
- North Temperate Zone
- Equatorial Zone, or the Tropics
- South Temperate Zone
- Antarctic Circle

Equatorial Zone

It is always hot in the equatorial zone (Aristotle called it the torrid zone), but there are two distinct seasons: a dry season and

🌍 GEO GEM

What's in a Day?
Were you taught that it takes 24 hours for the Earth to rotate on its axis? Actually, it takes 23 hours, 56 minutes, and 4 seconds. Astronomers call this a **sidereal day**. Fortunately, the sun moves each day, and that motion, combined with the Earth's rotation, gives us the 24 hours we call a day.

a wet season. This zone includes most of Africa, southern India, southern Asia, Indonesia, New Guinea, northern Australia, southern Mexico, Central America, and northern South America.

Temperate Zones

At the north and south temperate zones (between 23.5° latitude and 66° latitude north and south of the equator), the sun is never directly overhead, and the climate is mild, generally ranging from warm to cool. Of course, warm and cool are relative. In the winter the thermometer may hover in the single digits above and below 0°. In the summer the temperatures can exceed a "warm" 100°F (37.7°C). The temperate zones experience four annual seasons: spring, summer, autumn, and winter. The north temperate zone includes most of North America, as well as northern Mexico, Great Britain, Europe, and northern Asia. The south temperate zone includes southern Australia, New Zealand, southern South America, and southern Africa.

Frigid Zones

As the name suggests, the frigid zones are the coldest spots on planet Earth, mostly covered with ice and snow. The edge of the zone experiences one day at each solstice when the sun doesn't rise or set for 24 hours, while in the center of the zone (the pole), the day is literally one year long, with six months of daylight and six months of night. The north frigid zone (the Arctic) includes northern Canada and Alaska, Greenland, northern Scandinavia, and northern Russia. The continent of Antarctica is the only land within the south frigid zone (the Antarctic).

Climates Are Complicated

If climate were strictly defined by latitudes, it would be easy to understand. But the picture is complicated by other factors.

Prevailing Winds. Places nearer the equator receive more sunlight and are much warmer than places nearer the poles. The heat causes convection currents that rise and drive the general circulation of the atmosphere, transferring heat away from the equator toward the poles. The resulting wind belts are sometimes called prevailing winds. They blow more east-west than north-south due to the rotation of the Earth. The wind belts shift with the seasons, and so, too, do the climate zones.

Landmasses. Land surfaces react quickly to heat gain and loss, becoming warm in summer and cold in winter. Mountain ranges act as barriers to the movement of air. In North America prevailing west winds carrying moisture from the Pacific are blocked by the coastal ranges and the Sierras. As

AT THE BREAK OF DAY

As we consider longitude, let's not forget the **International Date Line**, yet another imaginary line on the globe. This one is 180° opposite the prime meridian and runs through the Pacific (with some wiggle around certain islands). On one side of the meridian is one date and, on the other, tomorrow—or yesterday—depending on whether you are traveling west or east.

the warm air rises, it cools; as it cools, it can't hold as much moisture, so rain falls. Consequently, on the east side of the mountain, conditions are much drier.

Elevation. As air rises, it cools. Therefore, as elevation increases, air temperature decreases. The vegetation on a typical mountain in the northern temperate forests will illustrate this principle dramatically. Mixed hardwood forests at lower elevations give way to evergreens, followed by alpine meadows of low-growing plants. Finally, at the peak there may be no vegetation at all, just rocks, often covered by snow and ice.

Oceans. The oceans gain and lose heat far more slowly than land. During the summer they are cooler than the adjoining land, while in winter they are warmer, affecting the land they border.

EL NIÑO

El niño is Spanish for "the little boy," meaning Jesus, because **El Niño** often appears around Christmastime, and the phenomenon is one of the world's most significant causes of extreme weather. Normally the trade winds in the Pacific blow from South America toward Asia. For some not yet fully understood reason, on occasions these winds fail. This means that the warm water that is usually piled up in the western equatorial Pacific spreads across to the east. The atmosphere receives more warm sea surface there to give it energy, and more evaporation means more moisture. As a result, the usual weather patterns are altered.

Some Impacts of El Niño
- Drought in Indonesia, Australia, and Malaysia
- Mild winters in northern United States and western Canada
- High rain in South America, leading to landslides along the Andes
- Heavy rainfall in Europe in spring, causing flooding

Currents circulate warm and cold water and affect the land nearby. The Gulf Stream in the Atlantic, for example, provides a warming influence on the weather of northwest Europe and the East Coast of the United States and Canada. The periodic El Niño current in the equatorial Pacific can have drastic consequences for the weather in parts of South America, Australia, and Asia (see box, opposite). Coastal regions generally experience mild and humid maritime climates, while the interiors of large landmasses have more continental climates, with warmer summers and colder winters.

While both the North and South poles are in frigid zones, the North Pole lies at sea level in the middle of the Arctic Ocean, which acts as a reservoir of heat. The North Pole averages a balmy –30°F (–34°C) in the winter. The summers are a comfortable 32°F (0°C). The South Pole sits atop a featureless, windswept, icy plateau at an altitude of 9,306 feet (2,836 m). The winter temperature at the South Pole remains steady at around –85°F (–65°C). The highest temperature ever recorded there, at the Amundsen-Scott South Pole Station, is 7.5°F (–13.6°C), and the lowest is a bone-chilling –117.0°F

All of the different climate influences interact. For example, prevailing winds in the Indian Ocean are northeasterly. During the summer months a large low-pressure system develops over southern Asia due to heating of the large interior landmass. This causes the winds from this region to change directions to form the southwest monsoons, bringing a prolonged wet season to Southeast Asia and the subcontinent of India.

CONTINENTS AND OCEANS

A continent is a large landmass. The world is divided into seven continents: North America, South America, Europe, Africa, Asia, Australia, and Antarctica. Did I say that Europe and Asia are two separate continents? The problem is, Europe and Asia form a single landmass divided by the Ural Mountains and the Caspian and Black seas. Russia and Turkey straddle that boundary line. Eurasia is a single landmass, but culturally it is considered two continents, and two continents it remains.

Continents account for just one-third of the surface of the Earth. The rest is ocean. There are four oceans: the Atlantic, Pacific, Indian, and Arctic. Did I say four? Since the year 2000, most geographers agree the area from the "shores" of Antarctica to where the Atlantic, Pacific, and Indian oceans join is a fifth ocean: the Southern Ocean.

THE EARTH FROM THE INSIDE OUT

The Earth is less solid than it looks. Seismologists currently think the inside of Earth has a solid **inner core,** made mostly of iron and estimated to be about 746 miles (2,400 km) in diameter. The temperature is extremely hot, estimated to be between 9000°F and 13,000°F (5,000°C and 7,000°C) and under pressure so high, the iron cannot melt.

Around the inner core is the **outer core,** a shell of liquid iron. This layer is the source of Earth's magnetic field and is about 1,400 miles (2,300 km) deep.

Next is the **mantle,** which is about 1,800 miles (2,900 km) thick and is separated into the upper and lower mantle. Large convective currents in the mantle circulate heat and may drive plate tectonic processes. Finally, there is a thin, brittle **crust,** which is where we live. It is between 22 and 44 miles (35 and 70 km) thick where the continents sit and between 3 and 6 miles (5 and 10 km) thick under the oceans.

Another way to look at the Earth is to consider its mechanical properties, or the causes of all the motion on the surface of the Earth in terms of earthquakes and volcanoes. From the inside out, you have the inner and outer cores as above. Then

THE FOUR LAYERS OF THE EARTH

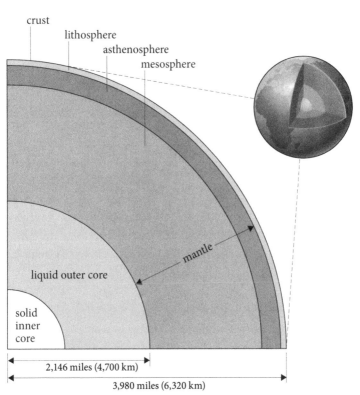

crust
lithosphere
asthenosphere
mesosphere

mantle

liquid outer core

solid
inner
core

2,146 miles (4,700 km)

3,980 miles (6,320 km)

you have the **mesosphere** (the bit of the mantle nearest the center of the Earth, outside the outer core), the **asthenosphere** (the semi-fluid layer whose movement allows the lithosphere to rise, fall, and move sideways), and the **lithosphere** (the rigid layer on the surface), which includes the **crust**.

How do we know all this, given that it adds up to a distance of just under 4,000 miles (6,400 km) from surface to core, and that digging down fewer than 8 of them required a massive national effort on the part of the U.S.S.R.? Well, geologists have pieced it together by measuring the behavior of seismic waves as they pass through the Earth and by studying the makeup of magma, lava, and escaping gases. That's the sort of thing geologists do.

Surrounding the crust is a gaseous layer that we call our **atmosphere**. Besides providing the oxygen-rich mix of air that all life depends on, the atmosphere protects us from the sun's dangerous radiation and allows weather systems to move, distributing heat and moisture around the planet.

YET ANOTHER LOOK AT THE PLANET

While we are at it, we might as well throw around some more terms. The area near the surface of the Earth can also be divided up four additional ways: the lithosphere, hydrosphere, biosphere, and atmosphere. All life on the planet happens in one of these **geospheres**.

Lithosphere. Consists of the rocky crust, which is composed of minerals and covers the entire surface of the Earth, from the mountaintops to the bottom of the ocean.

Hydrosphere. Composed of all of the water on the planet and in the atmosphere—as liquid, ice, and water vapor.

Biosphere. Comprises all living plants, animals, and one-celled organisms found above and below the ground and in the water.

Atmosphere. The body of air that surrounds our planet. The air of our planet is 79 percent nitrogen and just under 21 percent oxygen. The remaining 10 percent is composed of carbon dioxide and other gases.

CONTINENTAL DRIFT MEANS CONSTANT CHANGE

We live on a planet that is constantly changing. Most of the changes happen very slowly. Over hundreds of millions of years, the surface of the Earth has been continually reshaped as continents formed and broke up and formed again.

The shifting landforms are due to slowly shifting pieces of the Earth's crust, called tectonic plates. Convection currents deep within the Earth carry heat from the hot interior to the cooler surface, causing the plates on the surface to move. Even though the fastest plates move only a little over 2 inches (5 cm) a year, the accumulated force of their movements creates massive changes on the Earth's surface.

Gathering the Evidence

Over the course of the nineteenth century, explorers and scientists gathered evidence from all over the world that suggested the continents had not always been located where they are today. This evidence included:

Fossils. Mesosaurus are freshwater reptiles whose skeletons were found on both sides of the Atlantic. Either the skeletons had been dropped there by a passing pterodactyl or they crawled there on land. Forget the pterodactyls, because the dates don't work; the mesosaurus missed the pterodactyls by about 50 million years. Similarly, fossilized remains of other reptiles and the plant species *Glossopteris* across many continents added weight to the idea that the continents had once been joined.

Continental Fit. Back in the year 1620 Francis Bacon was possibly the first scholar to note that South America and Africa seemed to fit together like two pieces of a giant jigsaw puzzle. With modern satellite images this seems pretty obvious, but given the mapping that was available then, his finding was very impressive.

Climatology and Geology. Matching rock layers on either side of the Atlantic and the existence of coal seams in Antarctica clearly showed that there had either been some very severe shifts in climate patterns or that the places themselves had moved.

Drawing all this information together, a German astronomer and climatologist by the name of Alfred Wegener (1880–1930) postulated that in the beginning—perhaps 250 million years ago—there had been one supercontinent. In discussions centered on his work, scientists came up with the name **Pangaea** (Greek for "all land") to explain this phenomenon. This landmass later subdivided into a great northern continent called **Laurasia** and a great southern one called **Gondwanaland**. Laurasia eventually tore itself apart to produce North America, Europe, and Asia. Gondwanaland produced South America, Africa, India, Australia, and Antarctica.

TECTONIC PLATES ARE ON THE MOVE

We now know that Wegener was pretty much right and that the reason for the continental drift can be traced to the Earth's crust and mantle. To put it simply, the crust is not one solid whole; it is made up of plates—seven large plates and various sizes of smaller plates. **Oceanic plates** (those under the sea) are thinner and denser than **continental plates** (under the land). Telling which is which is not as simple as looking at where the seas are, though. Most continental plates extend beyond the shoreline, out of sight, beneath the water. The really important thing to know about these plates is that they move, and this means that the edges of one plate push up against the edges of another, with—it's hard not to say this—earth-shattering results.

 **GEO GEM**

B-r-r-r-r
Where's the coldest spot on the planet? Vostok Station, a Russian Antarctic research station, which holds the record with the lowest reliably measured temperature on Earth of −128.6°F (−89.2°C).

Where the Big Plates Are Heading

It is unsettling to know that the plates are always in motion and that they are all traveling in different directions, making rifts and collisions as inevitable as pile-ups on an icy highway.

- Antarctica plate: heading south
- African plate: heading southwest, away from Europe
- Eurasian plate: moving toward the southeast
- Indo-Australian plate: heading north
- North American plate: heading west
- South American plate: heading west

The Action Is at the Boundaries

Where one plate meets another, expect a lot of action. Below are the types of boundaries that exist, characterized by the way the plates move in relation to each other and the surface phenomena they create.

Constructive Boundaries. So-called because when magma rises from the mantle, it constructs, or creates, new crust, producing mid-ocean ridges, seamounts (undersea mountains), volcanoes, or volcanic islands.

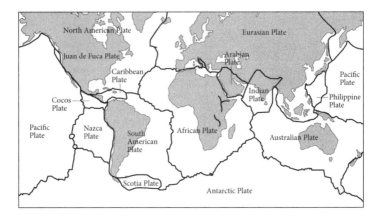

Destructive Boundaries. When heavier oceanic crust is drawn under continental crust, this produces deep sea trenches, island arcs, fold mountains, and more volcanoes.

Transform or Conservative Boundaries. When plates—which may be going in the same direction but at different speeds—rub past one another, local faulting or folding may occur, but no new landforms are created.

Constructive Plate Boundaries:
Iceland Shows Us How It's Done

North America is moving away from Europe at a rate of 2 inches (5 cm) per year. The reason can be found in the middle of the Atlantic. With a buckling up of the ocean floor, as well as magma rising and cooling to form great undersea mountain ranges and the occasional island, the landform features are quite clear. Such a fast rate of movement (2 inches/5 cm a year is actually fast) inevitably means there are earthquakes and, on occasion, surface-breaking volcanic activity associated with these boundaries.

Iceland exhibits the classic features created by constructive plate boundaries: tall volcanic peaks that have emerged from the sea to change from seamounts into islands. The most recent island created was **Surtsey**, off the southern coast. Between 1963 and 1968 a seamount repeatedly erupted until eventually the waters parted and a new volcanic island emerged—before the eyes of amazed Icelanders.

Destructive Plate Margins: Remember the Indonesian Tsunami of 2004?

Talk about destructive! Subduction is the name of the process creating landforms. Where continental shelf meets oceanic plate, there can be only one winner. The continental shelf is less dense than the oceanic plate, so the latter gets pushed (subducted) under the former—rather like a lightweight Ferrari hitting an armored tank. The oceanic plate breaks and buckles as it is driven under the continental shelf, resulting in shallow earthquakes. These earthquakes can produce deadly tsunami, like the one that struck the Indian Ocean in 2004.

As the subducted plate heads deep into the asthenosphere, it produces an **oceanic trench**. Being bent and heated as it goes, the subducted plate melts to form masses of igneous rock known as **plutons**. These plutons behave like wax globules in a lava lamp, rising through the crust, especially where the forces have created faults and cracks. Eventually, these

 **GEO GEM**

Ice Ages
The Earth's climate has experienced periods of extremely cold weather for such prolonged periods that much of the surface was covered in thick sheets of ice, wiping out thousands of species that were adapted to warmer weather. Humans survived the last Ice Age, but the woolly mammoth did not.

plutons create either seamounts off the coast of the continental plate or whole archipelagos, such as Japan.

The final landforms of note created by destructive plate boundaries are **fold mountains**. The greatest range of these runs from Canada to Tierra del Fuego and into Antarctica, including the Rocky Mountains in North America. While this is not quite a continuous range, it demonstrates the impact that subduction can have on the Earth's surface.

On occasions the heavily folded and faulted crust of fold mountains may allow plutons to rise and dot the range with volcanic peaks. Notable fold-mountain volcanoes include Mount Saint Helens in the Cascade range of the United States and Cotopaxi in Ecuador. If you are old enough to remember the 1980 eruption of Mount Saint Helens, you probably can recall the violence of this type of volcano, a characteristic of destructive plate margins.

Collision Mountains: The Himalayas Are Still Growing

The Himalayas were built by the collision of the massive Eurasian plate with the Indo-Australian plate. Both these plates have the same density, so they produce a head-on collision in which both crumple. The result? Mountains. B-i-i-i-g mountains. The Himalayas are still growing—at a rate of about 0.4 inches (1 cm) a year.

Transform Boundaries: California in the News

Constructive and destructive creation of landforms are dramatic, but the lowly transform fault is no slouch, either. It doesn't create any major landscape features, and it's very rare to have any volcanic activity. That doesn't mean there is nothing to worry about, though; the big news items here are earthquakes.

Easily the most studied and filmed transform fault area is in California, where the infamous San Andreas Fault is just one of many that marks the boundary between the North American and the Pacific plates. These two plates are moving in the same direction—northwest—but at different rates. The Pacific Plate moves at an average of 2½ inches (6.3 cm) per year, while the North American Plate moves at only about ½ inch (1.3 cm) per year. So on the surface there is a relative distancing of more than 2 inches (5 cm) a year. That is a lot of movement in plate-tectonic terms, and it is the reason this area is so prone to earthquakes.

CHANGING SURFACE FEATURES

But the drama doesn't all belong to plate tectonics. There's plenty of other forces that cause change to the Earth's surface,

A BRIEF TIME LINE OF THE EARTH

Below is a brief time line outlining some of the major events in the development of life on our planet. The dates are only estimates; new information continually forces science to revise the "facts."

4.6 billion years ago:	Earth formed, along with the other planets.
3.7 billion years ago:	Earth's crust solidified.
3.5 billion years ago:	First life appeared in oceans.
3.25 billion years ago:	Photosynthesis began in oceans.
1.9 billion years ago:	First cells with nuclei appeared in oceans.
1 billion years ago:	Plants and fungi appeared.
600 million years ago:	Simple animals started to appear.
500 million years ago:	Fish and early amphibians appeared.
475 million years ago:	Plants moved onto land.
300 million years ago:	Reptiles evolved on land.
245 million years ago:	Age of dinosaurs began.
200 million years ago:	Mammals appeared.
150 million years ago:	Supercontinent broke up, and birds took to the air.
65 million years ago:	Age of dinosaurs ended, with mass extinctions.
2.5 million years ago:	Early ancestors of man made an appearance.
100,000 years ago:	First Homo sapiens appeared.
10,000 years ago:	Recorded human history began.

🌐 GEO GEM

Oil Reserves

It is ironic that burning fossil fuels is implicated in global warming, since it was global warming that generated our reserves of fossil fuels. Periodic warming of the Earth during the Jurassic and Cretaceous periods created an abundance of plant and animal life. Where there is life, there are organic materials left behind to decay. Over millions of years this organic material built up undisturbed. It was eventually covered by sediment and compressed, giving us fossil fuels—coal, petroleum, and natural gas.

though they may happen on a smaller scale than the creation of mountain ranges. Rivers cut through land and create valleys and canyons—not that the Grand Canyon is small. Glaciers, which are rivers of ice, move across the land, dropping debris and carving out landforms, like the Great Lakes in North America—again, not a small landscape feature. Then there are everyday events, like landslides and floods, caused by excessive rain. In our lifetime, we may see rising ocean levels and the disappearance of certain islands due to climate change. Our planet is in a constant state of flux.

THE LIVING PLANET

Two thirds of the surface of the Earth is covered by water, and it was in the water that life began as a single-cell organism. Slowly the one-celled creatures formed large colonies, and gradually more complex life forms evolved. Photosynthesis developed, increasing the supply of oxygen in the oceans and making still more complex life forms possible. These complex life forms, both plants and animals, have spread and transformed the plant, creating grasslands and rain forests and arctic tundra as animals and plants have responded to the changing terrain and climates of Planet Earth.

Inhale, Then Exhale

One of the more interesting facts recently discovered by Charles David Keeling, a scientist from San Diego, is that the Earth breathes. Well, not quite. But in the process of measuring the amount of carbon dioxide in the atmosphere, Keeling discovered seasonal fluctuations in carbon dioxide levels. Since the Northern Hemisphere contains the greatest concentration of landmasses, and since much of that land experiences seasons, he theorized that plants were the basis of this fluctuation. The plants (trees, grasses, food crops, what have you) take up carbon dioxide as they sprout leaves and grow over the summer. When they shed the leaves in the fall, and the leaves die and decay in the winter, they release that carbon dioxide. Ours is a living, breathing planet.

Chapter 2

Water, Water Everywhere

Although ancient sailors supposedly sailed the "seven seas" to travel around the world, in truth the globe is encircled by just five oceans (in order of size): Pacific, Atlantic, Indian, Arctic, and Southern.

As noted in Chapter 1, you may not have heard of that last ocean. The presence of a fifth ocean has been subject to debate among scientists for a while. In the spring of 2000, the International Hydrographic Organization, an agency that studies the world's waters and is recognized by most nations, decided that the waters surrounding Antarctica north to where the Pacific, Atlantic, and Indian oceans converge is a fifth world ocean, named the Southern Ocean.

PEACEFUL WATERS: THE PACIFIC OCEAN

This vast body of water was named by Ferdinand Magellan in 1519 on his famous trip around the world, because he felt

 **GEO GEM**

Too cold to swim in?
The average water temperature of the combined oceans is about 39°F (2°C).

the Pacific was a peaceful ocean. But once you get below the surface, you'll see that the Pacific is anything but. Hundreds of tropical storms batter its surface annually, the rim is lined with vol-canoes, and tsunamis—underwater earthquakes—have destroyed entire villages. Below are some remarkable facts that pertain to this mysterious cosmic sea.

- It is the largest ocean, covering more than a third of the Earth's surface.
- It contains more than half of the Earth's water.
- It provides the greatest amount of the world's fish supply.
- It contains the notorious **Ring of Fire**, an arc of intense seismic (earthquake) and volcanic activity stretching from New Zealand, along the eastern edge of Asia, north across the Aleutian Islands of Alaska, and south along the coast of North and South America. More than 75 percent of the world's volcanoes lie within this ring.
- It contains the deepest spot on the surface of the Earth, the **Mariana Trench**, just east of Guam. It was formed by one oceanic plate being pushed below another in a process known as **subduction**.
- Within the Mariana Trench is **Challenger Deep**, about 36,000 feet (11,000 m) below sea level. (If you were able to pick up and move Mount Everest, the highest mountain on Earth, and place it on this spot, it wouldn't even break the surface of the water; there would be about 1 mile/1.6 km of ocean concealing it.)

THE YOUNGEST OCEAN: THE ATLANTIC

The youngest of the oceans, the Atlantic was formed when the supercontinent Pangaea broke apart. As the western and eastern landmasses drew apart, a great rift was formed, creating the Atlantic Ocean basin. The ocean separates North and South America from Europe and Africa and extends from the Arctic almost to Antarctica. Here are some interesting tidbits about this ocean that reveal that, although smaller and younger than the Pacific, the Atlantic is just as extraordinary—and just as fierce.

- It is the second largest ocean.
- It includes the Baltic Sea, North Sea, Black Sea, and Mediterranean Sea to the east; to the west it includes Hudson Bay, the Gulf of St. Lawrence, Gulf of Mexico, and Caribbean Sea.
- In the North much of the Atlantic is covered in **sea ice,** and **icebergs** pose a hazard for ships that travel its waters.
- **Hurricanes** are another hazard of the Atlantic. From June 1 to November 30, tropical storms form off the coast of Africa and cross the Atlantic, taking up vast amounts of moisture. The storms blow over the Caribbean, coastal areas of the Gulf of Mexico, and the southern Atlantic coast of the United States, with damaging winds, devastating amounts of rain, and storm surges.
- Waters from many of the world's **largest rivers** flow into the

🌐 GEO GEM

I Fell into a Burning Ring of Fire

Ninety percent of all volcanic activity occurs in the oceans. The largest known concentration of active volcanoes is in the South Pacific.

🌐 GEO GEM

Climb Every Mountain
The Earth's longest mountain range is the undersea Mid-Ocean Ridge, which is about 40,000 miles (64,000 km) long—four times longer than the Andes, Rockies, and Himalayas combined. It winds around the globe from the Arctic Ocean to the Atlantic, skirting continents and crossing the Pacific to the west coast of North America.

Atlantic, including the Amazon, Congo, and Niger rivers. The Nile flows into the Mediterranean Sea, which is considered part of the Atlantic.

- The warm **Gulf Stream** of the Atlantic Ocean flows past the shores of Northern Europe, moderating the climate and keeping the harbors free from ice during winter.
- The Atlantic Ocean causes the **highest tides** in the world, which occur in the Bay of Fundy, Canada, with a rise of around 50 feet (15 m) in the spring tides.
- The cold **Labrador Current** off Newfoundland carries icebergs southward, one of which was responsible for the Atlantic's most famous shipwreck, the *Titanic*.
- The largest island in the Atlantic Ocean is **Greenland**. The most famous island in the Atlantic is the one that never existed—the lost island of **Atlantis**.
- The newest island in the Atlantic is **Surtsey**, formed off the coast of Iceland in 1963.

TROPICAL WATERS: THE INDIAN OCEAN

The Indian Ocean takes its name from India, which it borders. This ocean reaches average surface temperatures of 72°F (22°C) in the northern parts. In the southern part of the ocean, below 20° latitude, temperatures are much lower. Most think of the disastrous Indonesian Tsunami of 2004 when they think of the

Indian Ocean. This was due to an earthquake under its waters that generated waves recorded at a height of 49 feet (14.9 m).

Here are some other interesting facts:

- The **Arabian Sea**, **Persian Gulf**, and **Red Sea** are all part of the Indian Ocean.
- Forty percent of the world's **offshore oil drilling** takes place here.
- The Bay of Bengal is sometimes called **Cyclone Alley** because of all the storms that begin there.
- Changing air-pressure systems over the Indian Ocean trigger the famous **monsoon season** of Asia.
- The Indian Ocean contains some of the world's most popular tropical island destinations. The countless islands of the **Maldives** and the **Seychelles** feature some of the most inviting beaches in the world.
- The **Maldive Islands**, at 8 feet (2.4 m) above sea level at their highest point, are expected to be the first casualties of **rising sea levels** caused by **global warming**.

A Sea of Ice: The Arctic Ocean

Much of the Arctic Ocean lies north of the Arctic Circle and has historically been a sea of ice. That may be changing due to global warming. Besides being the smallest and shallowest of the world's five major oceans, here are some other specifics:

- It is bounded on all sides by North America, Europe, and Asia.

🌎 GEO GEM

Coasting Along

Canada has the longest coastline of any country, at 56,453 miles (90,852 km), or about 15 percent of the world's 372,384 miles (599,293 km) of coastlines.

- During winter, the Arctic Ocean historically has been almost completely covered in sea ice.
- For centuries explorers tried to find the **Northwest Passage**, a route through the Arctic Ocean from the Atlantic to the Pacific, but none succeeded. Today ice-breaking ships travel ahead of the trade ships sailing on the Arctic Ocean, making a path through the ice.

NEW GUY ON THE GLOBE: THE SOUTHERN OCEAN

The existence of the Southern Ocean hasn't been universally acknowledged, but more than ever, geographic and oceanographic agencies are making its presence official. It is also known as the Great Southern Ocean, the Antarctic Ocean, and the South Polar Ocean, and it extends from the coast of Antarctica north to 60° south latitude.

The waters of the ocean are divided into two different temperature zones. The **Antarctic Convergence** is a curve continuously encircling Antarctica where cold, northward-flowing Antarctic waters meet the relatively warmer waters of the subantarctic. The cold Antarctic waters sink beneath the warmer water, creating an actively moving and mixing zone where marine life thrives, especially Antarctic krill. This natural boundary separates areas of different climates. The **Antarctic Circumpolar Current** (ACC) flows from west to east around Antarctica and is the strongest ocean current in the world. By preventing warm ocean waters from reaching Antarctica, it enables that continent to maintain its huge ice sheet.

The Southern Ocean is subject to all the same international treaties as the rest of the world's oceans. Additionally, there are some international agreements that restrict activities in the Southern Ocean. The International Whaling Commission prohibits commercial whaling south of 40° south latitude;

IS THE DEAD SEA REALLY DEAD?
Depends on what you mean by "dead." Certainly, it is too salty to support much marine life, though it does support swimmers who can float easily in the water.

the Convention on the Conservation of Antarctic Seals limits sealing; the Convention on the Conservation of Antarctic Marine Living Resources regulates fishing. Also, many nations, including the United States, prohibit mineral resource exploration and exploitation south of the Antarctic Convergence.

THE SEVEN SEAS

And what about those seas? For the most part, seas are named parts of oceans, though some are actually saltwater lakes, like the Caspian Sea and the Dead Sea. There aren't seven seas; there are hundreds of them.

But let's not forget the **Persian Gulf** in the Indian Ocean. Small in size but rich in oil reserves, this little sea generates more column inches of news than any other sea in the world.

WHAT LIES BENEATH

The surface of the ocean doesn't give many clues to the amazing landscape of the ocean floor. It's only recently that mapping the floor of the ocean has been attempted. Here are a few of the things they are finding.

Continental Shelves: Land sloping gently under the water around the continents

Abyssal Plain: Large area of extremely flat or gently sloping ocean floor just beyond the continental shelves and known as some of the flattest spots on Earth

Ocean ridges: Long mountain ranges

Long rift valleys: Where earthquakes and volcanic eruptions are common

Seamounts: Isolated mountains

Guyots: Extinct volcanoes with flat tops

Ocean Trenches: The deepest parts of the oceans

Volcanoes: Rise from the ridges that may appear above the surface as islands

Geothermal vents: Hot spots

MARINE LIFE

The ocean provides a variety of habitats for ocean creatures and plants, and life in the ocean is incredibly diverse. It ranges from microscopic bacteria to the largest mammal on Earth—the enormous blue whale, which can grow to 110 feet (34 m)

WHY IS THE OCEAN SALTY?

Oceans are salty because fresh water flows into them. Okay, that answer is impossibly counterintuitive, but freshwater flow *is* the major contributor of salt. The original oceans were probably only slightly salty. Over millennia, rivers flowed over the newly formed land, carving out canyons, dissolving mountains, and picking up lots of dissolved minerals (salt). These dissolved minerals all end up flowing into the ocean.

Meanwhile, the ocean surface is heated by the sun, causing water to evaporate. What's left behind are those dissolved minerals—a cycle that continues through today. Over time the oceans became salty from the continued inflow of dissolved minerals. The Atlantic Ocean, repository of the greatest river water flow, is the saltiest of the oceans.

in length. Some of these animals are migratory, traveling huge distances from spawning grounds to feeding grounds, while other critters stay in the same place on the ocean floor their entire lives. Some burrow beneath the sand, while others

THE 10 LARGEST SEAS

NAME	LOCATION	SIZE (SQ. MI.)
South China Sea	In the Pacific, between mainland Asia and the Philippines	1,148,500
Caribbean Sea	In the Atlantic, east of Central America	1,068,000
Mediterranean Sea	In the Atlantic, between Europe and Africa	971,000
Bering Sea	At the very north of the Pacific, between Alaska and Russia	875,000
Gulf of Mexico	In the Atlantic, south of the eastern United States, east of Mexico	596,000
Sea of Okhotsk	In the Pacific, south of eastern Russia, north of Japan	590,000
East China & Yellow Sea	In the Pacific, east of mainland China, north of South China, and south of the Okhotsk	482,000
Sea of Japan	In the Pacific, between Japan and eastern Asia	389,000
North Sea	In the Atlantic, east of Great Britain, bounded on the east by Denmark	220,000
Black Sea	In the Atlantic, surrounded by Eastern Europe, Russia, and Turkey	178,000

swim near the surface. Scientists believe that there may be as many as 10 million species of plants and animals in the ocean that no one has ever seen, much less named.

Most of the diverse marine life lives in the top layer of the ocean, where sunlight can penetrate but where the ocean temperatures are relatively cool. In this environment phytoplankton, algae, and plants like sea grass make their own food through the process of photosynthesis and are at the bottom of most marine food chains.

There are basically four geographic zones for marine life:

Intertidal Zone. Where the ocean meets the land. Many animals, plants, and algae make their homes between the low-tide and high-tide levels

Open Ocean. The largest marine ecosystem, home to swimming fish, drifting plankton, and other creatures

Shallow Ocean Floor. A sunlit floor in which animals, plants, and algae thrive

Deep Ocean. An extreme environment tolerated by highly adapted species

Fisheries

The oceans are an important source of food, accounting for about 16 percent of the animal protein consumed annually, but the amount of fish consumed varies by region. Researchers have found that about 75 percent of the major marine fish stocks are either depleted, overexploited, or being fished at their biological limits. Pollution, habitat destruction, and global warming are also contributing to their demise.

Populations of commercially attractive large fish, such as tuna, cod, swordfish, and marlin, have declined by as much as 90 percent in the past century. Species of fish endangered by

TSUNAMI

Along with landslides, tsunamis are the most significant secondary natural killers triggered by earthquakes. The catastrophic tsunami that struck the Indian Ocean in December 2004 killed about 275,950 people, according to the U.S. Geological Survey. Tsunamis can result from an underwater earthquake, underwater volcanic eruption, underwater landslide, or landslide into water.

The largest recorded tsunami measured 210 feet (64 m) above sea level when it reached Siberia's Kamchatka Peninsula in 1737.

overfishing are tuna, salmon, haddock, halibut, and cod. In the nineteenth century, codfish weighing up to 200 pounds were not uncommon; today a 40-pound cod is considered huge.

Life on the Ocean Floor

Most of the fisheries and marine ecosystems are near the water surface, dependent on solar energy for photosynthesis. Below a depth of about 660 feet (200 m), not enough sunlight penetrates to allow photosynthesis to occur. The relatively shallow penetration of solar energy and the sinking of cold, subpolar water combine to make most of the deep ocean floor a frigid environment with few life forms. However, geothermal hot springs along the spreading centers of mid-ocean ridges provide dissolved minerals and heat to specially adapted bacteria that use chemosynthesis rather than photosynthesis. These special bacteria form the basis of an ecosystem that supports a surprising diversity of marine life that can thrive in densities of up to 65 pounds (29 kg) per square foot. Among them are giant tubeworms and mussels.

Chapter 3

North America

Vast and diverse, the North American continent stretches from the Arctic Circle south through Panama at the northern tip of South America, just 500 miles (800 km) north of the equator. Surrounded on three sides by ocean (Arctic, Atlantic, and Pacific), North America boasts many islands offshore, including Greenland, the world's largest island. Water and other natural resources are abundant. The sheer variety of environments— Arctic tundra, grasslands, temperate forest, desert, and rain forest—means an incredible variety of plants and animals, too. Massive glaciers, rugged mountains, desert mesas, sweeping prairies, white-sand beaches, sharp-sided canyon lands—the North American continent has all that and more.

POLITICAL DIVISIONS OF NORTH AMERICA

With Canada the second largest country in the world in terms of area, and the United States right behind it, North America is dominated by the countries at its northern end. These two countries drive the economy of North America, whose people enjoy the highest income per capita of any on the planet. Off the coast of Canada is Greenland, which is not an independent nation; it is a protectorate of Denmark.

To the south, the North American continent includes Mexico, the seven nations of the Central America subcontinent, the Caribbean, West Indies, and dozens of territories

THE 23 NATIONS OF THE NORTH AMERICAN CONTINENT

COUNTRY	CAPITAL	AREA*	POPULATION**
Antigua & Barbuda	St. John's	0.2	0.10
Bahamas	Nassau	5.0	0.30
Barbados	Bridgetown	0.2	0.30
Belize	Belmopan	9.0	0.30
Canada	Ottawa	3,850.0	33.50
Costa Rica	San José	20.0	4.30
Cuba	Havana	43.0	11.50
Dominica	Roseau	0.3	0.10
Dominican Republic	Santo Domingo	19.0	9.70
El Salvador	San Salvador	8.0	7.20
Grenada	St. George's	0.1	0.10
Guatemala	Guatemala City	42.0	13.30

and possessions—23 nations in all, 9.5 million square miles (24,500,000 sq km), and 530 million people.

FROM SEA TO SHINING SEA: THE VAST LAND

One way to look at a continent is to study its landforms. These landforms tell us something about the forces that formed the landscape and shaped how people live on the land. North America can be divided into several regions

Haiti	Port-au-Prince	11.0	9.00
Honduras	Tegucigalpa	43.0	7.80
Jamaica	Kingston	4.0	2.80
Mexico	Mexico City	756.0	111.20
Nicaragua	Managua	50.0	5.90
Panama	Panama City	29.0	3.40
Saint Kitts & Nevis	Basseterre	0.1	0.04
Saint Lucia	Castries	0.2	0.20
Saint Vincent & the Grenadines	Kingstown	0.2	0.10
Trinidad & Tobago	Port-of-Spain	2.0	1.20
United States	Washington, D.C.	3,718.0	307.20

*in thousands of square miles
**in millions

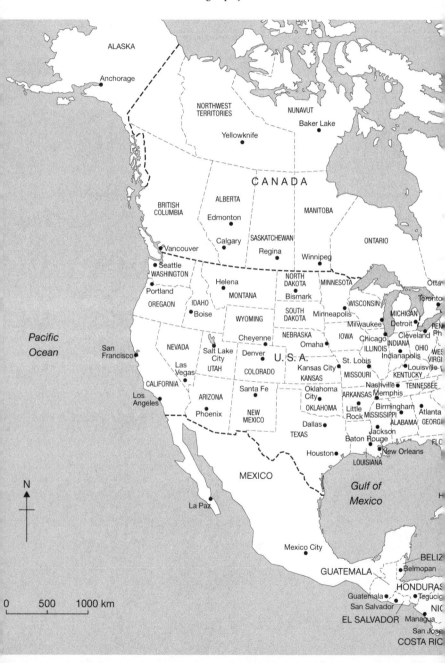

based on their physical and geographic features.

Atlantic–Gulf Coastal Plain. A flat coastal plain stretches along the shores of the Atlantic Ocean and the Gulf of Mexico, from Cape Cod all the way west and south to Mexico. It runs through most of Florida and extends southeast of Florida to form the Bahama Islands. In the Northeast, portions of the plain are quite narrow, but at its widest it extends from the mouth of the Mississippi in Louisiana all the way up to southern Illinois. Capes (Cape Cod, Cape Hatteras), sandy beaches, estuaries, and barrier islands are all features of the coastal plain. If you are thinking that tourism is important to the coastal plains, you are correct. The coastal plain also includes many fine natural harbors, including those of New York Bay and Chesapeake Bay, the presence of which influenced colonial settlement patterns and boosted the economies of those areas.

Appalachian Highlands. A transitional zone of foothills, the highlands (sometimes called the **Piedmont**) stretch from New Jersey to central Alabama. The foothills give way to a series of parallel north–south running mountain ridges lying between plateaus. These ancient

(continued on page 54)

THE 50 U.S. STATES AND THEIR CAPITALS

STATE	NICKNAME	CAPITAL
Alabama	Yellowhammer State	Montgomery
Alaska	Last Frontier	Juneau
Arizona	Grand Canyon State	Phoenix
Arkansas	Natural State	Little Rock
California	Golden State	Sacramento
Colorado	Centennial State	Denver
Connecticut	Nutmeg State	Hartford
Delaware	First State	Dover
Florida	Sunshine State	Tallahassee
Georgia	Peach State	Atlanta
Hawaii	Aloha State	Honolulu
Idaho	Gem State	Boise
Illinois	Prairie State	Springfield
Indiana	Hoosier State	Indianapolis
Iowa	Hawkeye State	Des Moines
Kansas	Sunflower State	Topeka
Kentucky	Bluegrass State	Frankfort
Louisiana	Pelican State	Baton Rouge

STATE	NICKNAME	CAPITAL
Maine	Pine Tree State	Augusta
Maryland	Old Line State	Annapolis
Massachusetts	Bay State	Boston
Michigan	Wolverine State	Lansing
Minnesota	North Star State	Saint Paul
Mississippi	Magnolia State	Jackson
Missouri	Show-me State	Jefferson City
Montana	Treasure State	Helena
Nebraska	Cornhusker State	Lincoln
Nevada	Silver State	Carson City
New Hampshire	Granite State	Concord
New Jersey	Garden State	Trenton
New Mexico	Land of Enchantment	Santa Fe
New York	Empire State	Albany
North Carolina	Tar Heel State	Raleigh
North Dakota	Peace Garden State	Bismarck
Ohio	Buckeye State	Columbus
Oklahoma	Sooner State	Oklahoma City

THE 50 U.S. STATES AND THEIR CAPITALS *(continued)*

STATE	NICKNAME	CAPITAL
Oregon	Beaver State	Salem
Pennsylvania	Keystone State	Harrisburg
Rhode Island	Ocean State	Providence
South Carolina	Palmetto State	Columbia
South Dakota	Mount Rushmore	Pierre
Tennessee	Volunteer State	Nashville
Texas	Lone Star State	Austin
Utah	Beehive State	Salt Lake City
Vermont	Great Mountain State	Montpelier
Virginia	The Old Dominion	Richmond
Washington	Evergreen State	Olympia
West Virginia	Mountain State	Charleston
Wisconsin	Badger State	Madison
Wyoming	Equality State	Cheyenne

NOTE: The District of Columbia is not a state but a federal district. Its boundaries are the same as those of the city of Washington, an area of 61 square miles (98 sq km). It is most commonly referred to as Washington, D.C. It is worth noting, also, that Hawaii is technically not part of North America. It is grouped with Australia and the other Pacific Islands. Who knew?

Texans may boast that everything is bigger in the Lone Star State, but Alaska, at around 570,000 square miles (92,000 sq km), is more than twice the size of Texas (262,000 square miles/422,000 sq km). Texas is 1.6 times the size of California (164,000 square miles/264,000 sq km), but its population lags behind. As of the 2010 Census, fastest-growing Texas has a population of more than 25 million, while California leads with more than 37 million.

CANADIAN PROVINCES AND TERRITORIES

PROVINCE	NICKNAME	CAPITAL
British Columbia	Pacific Province	Victoria
Alberta	Princess Province	Edmonton
Saskatchewan	Wheat Province	Regina
Manitoba	Keystone Province	Winnipeg
Ontario	Heartland Province	Toronto
Quebec	La Belle Province	Quebec
New Brunswick	Loyalist Province	Fredericton
Nova Scotia	Canada's Ocean Playground	Halifax
Prince Edward Island	Garden Province	Charlottetown
Newfoundland & Labrador	The Rock	Saint John's
TERRITORIES*	NICKNAME	CAPITAL
Yukon	Land of the Midnight Sun	Whitehorse
Northwest Territories	Land of the Polar Bear	Yellowknife
Nunavut	(no nickname)	Iquluit

*Yukon and the Northwest Territories have been part of the Canadian federation since shortly after the country became a self-governing dominion in 1867. Until 1999, Nunavut was part of the Northwest Territories.

🌐 GEO GEM

Confused?

Dominica and the Dominican Republic are two nations that are easily confused. Dominica is one of the Lesser Antilles islands in the southeastern Caribbean. The Dominican Republic, farther north but still in the Caribbean, shares the island of Hispaniola with Haiti and forms part of the Greater Antilles.

mountains were formed when the plate boundaries of North America and Africa collided during the formation of Pangaea, the supercontinent. That makes the mountains about 300 million years old. It's no surprise that weather and erosion have smoothed and softened the contours of the mountains over the millenia. If it were not for various uplifting geographical events, the Appalachian mountains would have disappeared long ago.

Interior Lowlands. Once covered by an inland sea, what is often called the American Midwest is a vast expanse of rolling land that stretches from the Appalachians to the Rocky Mountains. It includes the Canadian provinces of Alberta, Saskatchewan, and Manitoba and rolls south all the way to Texas. Cereal cropland of the agricultural heartland on the east gives way to cattle ranching on the west, where the Great Plains, a treeless plateau, gently rises to the foothills of the Rocky Mountains.

Rocky Mountain System. The geologically youthful Rockies is not one but several mountain ranges grouped together. Compared to the Appalachian Mountains, the Rockies are dramatically rugged and tall. The range starts in Alaska, runs through Canada and the United States, and on south to South America. In Mexico the mountains are called the

Sierra Madre; in Central America the Central Highlands. The **Continental Divide** is located in the Rocky Mountains and designates the line at which waters flow either to the Atlantic or Pacific oceans.

Intermountain Region. The derivation of this name is pretty obvious, because it is the region that lies between the Rockies on the East and the Cascades and Sierra Nevadas on the West and extends south into Mexico with the Mexican Plateau. What isn't obvious is the spectacular scenery it possesses. The Grand Canyon, the red-and-purple sandstone cliffs of the Canyonlands in Utah, and the great Salt Lake are all part of this arid and semiarid region. High mesas, isolated mountains, and desert basins are characteristic of the area.

The Pacific Mountain System. Bordering the Pacific Ocean, a series of volcanic mountain ranges, including the Cascades and Sierra Nevada, gives drama to the West Coast scenery. The northern reaches of this system parallel Alaska's southern coast and rise to **Mount McKinley**, also called **Denali**, the highest peak of North America at 20,3240 feet (6,194 m). The islands of southeast Alaska and those of the Aleutian Islands chain are partially submerged portions of the Pacific Mountain System and frequently experience volcanic activity and earthquakes. The coastline of the Pacific has only three good harbors: San Diego Bay, San Francisco Bay, and Puget Sound.

 **GEO GEM**

Not on the List

Two familiar names that didn't make it into the list of nations of North America are Puerto Rico, an "unincorporated territory" of the United States, subject to federal law, and Bermuda, a partially self-governing British overseas territory.

Canadian Shield. Also called the **Laurentian Plateau**, this area covers all of Greenland, about half of Canada, and extends into the United States, including the Adirondacks, northern Michigan, northern Wisconsin, and northern Minnesota. The landscape was shaped by the retreat of the last Ice Age, which scoured the land to expose ancient rocks and left behind hundreds of lakes.

The Antillean System. South of the Rocky and Pacific mountains, these mountains extend east and southeast from southern Mexico through Central America and the islands of the Antilles. The highest peaks are in the west and include active volcanoes.

FROM FROSTY TO STEAMY: CLIMATES

Climate is a complicated subject. The oceans, elevations, prevailing winds, and distance from the North Pole or equator all factor in to define the varied climates of North America. The presence of the Rocky Mountains and, to a lesser extent, the Appalachians, prevents moisture from the oceans from reaching the interior of the continent. The lack of mountains running east to west allows polar air to sweep in to affect the northeastern parts. Although the climate range includes the extremes, a substantial proportion of the continent is quite temperate.

Arctic. Very few hearty souls live in the far northern parts of North America, where the extreme cold of winter lasts through six months of darkness. Parts of the land are covered by a permanent ice cap. Greenland and far northern Canada have an arctic climate. A climate that is satisfying to polar bears is rarely conducive to population growth.

Subarctic. A subarctic climate is very, very cold, but at least it has some summer. There is at least one month, and sometimes three months, of above-freezing temperatures in parts of northern Canada and northern Alaska.

Humid Continental. The northeastern United States and southeastern parts of Canada have four distinct seasons, with warm and humid summers and cold and snowy winters.

Semiarid. The wide-open middle of the continent is semiarid, neither desert nor moist, but somewhere in between. This climate is also called a steppe climate. In the United States the semiarid climate supports grasslands and is prone to natural disasters, such as floods, lighting, tornadoes, and hail.

Desert. Parts of the American Southwest and Central America receive so little rain, they qualify

GEO GEM

North America's
Largest Coral Reef
Belize boasts the second-longest coral barrier reef in the world, but at a mere 200 miles (322 km) it is dwarfed by Australia's Great Barrier Reef (1,600 miles/2,575 km).

🌐 GEO GEM

A Danger Zone
Most of Central America rests on the small but geologically active Caribbean Plate, accounting for the region's numerous deadly earthquakes and volcanoes.

as deserts. As such, they experience significant daytime and nightime temperature variations.

Humid Subtropical. In the American South, excluding southern Florida, the summers are hot and humid and the winters are mostly mild. Rainfall is even throughout the year, and thunderstorms and tornadoes are also common.

Tropical. Central America, the islands of the Caribbean, and southern Florida have a tropical climate, which means it is hot year-round, with more precipitation in winter than in summer. The area is vulnerable to hurricanes.

Highland. Temperature and precipitation in the Rockies depend on elevation and local geography.

Mediterranean. It should come as no surprise that the wine-growing regions of central and southern California have a Mediterranean climate, with mild, moist winters and hot, dry summers.

Marine Coast. Along the coast of California, ocean currents are cold. The cold water is responsible for the fog and rain of northern California that continues on up to Canada.

THE PEOPLE OF NORTH AMERICA

We can quickly dispense with the notion that Christopher Columbus "discovered" America. The first human inhabitants of North America crossed over to Alaska on a land-bridge from northeastern Asia roughly 20,000 years ago and then moved southward. About 1,000 years ago Norsemen settled in Greenland and probably eastern Canada shortly thereafter.

Columbus started a second wave of European migration when he explored the Bahamas, West Indies, and Central America in the late 1400s. The floodgates were then opened to English, French, and Spanish explorers, who were soon followed by settlers.

The Europeans brought disease and war to the New World, decimating the native populations. Soon enough the population of Canada and the United States could be described as largely of European origin. Today it is growing increasingly diverse with substantial immigration from Asia, Latin America, and Africa.

The Inuit, thought to be of Asian descent, are the largest group of people in the Arctic. Most of their villages are located in coastal areas, where they fish and hunt seal, caribou, and whales. The Inuit used to be known as Eskimos. More than four-fifths of the population of Greenland are also Inuit, with a small number of people descended from early European settlers. The remainder are Danes.

The original indigenous Amerindian population of Central America and the Caribbean make up about 20 percent of the population today, and only in Guatemala do they form a significant portion of the population. The greatest majority of people, approximately 60 percent, are of mixed European, African, and Amerindian descent. Those of strictly European ancestry make up approximately 12 percent, with the remainder of Asian descent from Chinese and East Indian indentured servants.

THE GREAT ATLANTIC COD

Although there's no question that some settlers came to North America seeking religious freedom, many came for economic gain. For some of North America's early settlers, nothing was more important than cod.

The Grand Banks on the continental shelf off Newfoundland was particularly rich in fish due to a unique combination of geographic features. In the relatively shallow water found there, the cold Labrador Current mixes with the warm waters of the Gulf Stream, lifting nutrients to the surface and providing abundant food for the Atlantic cod. Basque and Portuguese boats fished those waters well before Columbus's famous "discovery" of the New World.

Why was cod so important? Because it was tasty in its dried, salted form, which meant it was a nutritious, long-lasting, affordable food. The dominant Catholic Church in Europe required that no meat be eaten on certain days of the year (including every Friday), and salt cod was available even where there was no fresh-caught fish. So it became an extremely important trade item from the 1500s through the collapse of the Grand Banks fishery in modern times.

In colonial North America the British used small boats close to shore, catching the cod with hook and line. To preserve the fish for transport back to England, they dried and salted the fish on land, a process that required settlements

WHAT IS A DESERT?

Even though we know a desert when we see one, there are parameters that define a desert climate, starting with less than 10 inches (25 cm) of accumulated moisture (rain or snow) annually. The dryness of desert air creates a situation where more moisture is evaporated from plants and the ground than actually accumulates during the year. Low moisture in the air allows more sunlight to reach the ground, raising daytime temperatures, another distinguishing feature of a desert.

of shore-based workers. English colonists settled in numbers along the Atlantic Coast to support this industry. Meanwhile, the French processed their catch with salt aboard ship and were not at all dependent on settling people in the New World. This is reflected today in the dominance of the English language and culture in the Canadian provinces of New Foundland and New Brunswick and in the New England region of the United States.

The North American colonists grew wealthy from the trade of salt cod for molasses to make rum in a triangle of trade with both England and British Caribbean—a little too wealthy, in the opinion of the English court. In 1733 Britain tried to gain control over that trade by imposing the Molasses Act. The thought was that the tax would eliminate the trade by making it unprofitable. Instead, the cod trade grew because the French were eager to work with the New Englanders. The American settlers traded cod with the French Caribbean, and the increase in trade benefited the American market. Eventually, the New England settlers were organized into a "codfish aristocracy," wealthy merchants interested in protecting their

GEO GEM

Peninsulas: Think Florida and More

A **peninsula** is an extension of land surrounded by water on three sides. A peninsula can also be a headland, cape, promontory, or spit. Besides Florida, North America has the Labrador Peninsula, which includes all of the province of Labrador and most of Quebec in Canada; Cape Cod in Massachusetts; and the Baja California peninsula in Mexico, a long finger stretching out from California. The Yucatan Peninsula partly separates the Gulf of Mexico from the Caribbean Sea.

trade. It was members of this codfish aristocracy that insti-
gated the famous Boston Tea Party.

The Treaty of Paris, which ended the American Revolution,
established the independence of the United States, gave England
dominion over all the lands of Canada, and yielded certain
fishing rights to the French. One British aristocrat, William Pitt
the Elder, criticizing the treaty in Parliament, claimed that cod
was "British gold" and that it was folly to restore Newfoundland
fishing rights to the French. But so it went.

THE DUST BOWL: A COMBINATION
OF HUMAN ERROR AND BAD WEATHER

The vast grasslands of North America function as the "breadbasket
of the world," but ecological disaster in the 1930s threatened to turn
that productive region into a "dust bowl." How did that happen?

The problem began during World War I, when farmers
responded to the high price of wheat and the needs of Allied
troops by plowing up and seeding marginal land that was
previously used only for grazing. After the war, livestock were
returned to graze on this land, and their hooves pulverized the bare
soil, which was no longer held in place by the extensive roots of
the native grasses.

Meanwhile, unstable sea-surface temperatures caused by cooler
than normal tropical Pacific Ocean temperatures and warmer
than normal tropical Atlantic Ocean temperatures created drought
conditions. The result was dry air and high temperatures in the
Midwest from about 1931 to 1939. In 1934 strong winds blew the
soil into huge clouds called "dusters" or "black blizzards." The dust
storms recurred in the ensuing years, ruining crops and pasturelands.
Complete disaster was averted through the adoption of plowing
patterns that countered prevailing winds, thus avoiding wind erosion.
A shift in weather patterns helped, too.

The codfish stocks for the Grand Banks are severely depleted today from overfishing. The necessity of restricting catches to avoid extinction of the cod is a major political issue, which runs up against opposition from the fishing industry and politicians reluctant to approve any measures that will result in job losses.

 **GEO GEM**

The Very Tip of North America
The Isthmus of Panama connects North America to South America. An isthmus is a narrow strip of land with water on both sides that connects two large land areas.

NATURAL RESOURCES OF NORTH AMERICA

Blessed with a vast amount of land within the temperate climate zone and abundant resources, North America is an agricultural powerhouse. It produces most of the world's corn, meat, soybeans, tobacco, and wheat, along with a variety of other food.

The Rocky Mountain region is rich in copper, lead, gold, silver, tungsten, uranium, and zinc. Coal, petroleum, and natural gas are fossil fuels found throughout the continent and offshore, though its accessibility varies considerably.

Chapter 4

South America

South America is a continent of contrasts—high mountains and river basins, desert and rainforest, savannah lands and cloud forest, tropics and glaciers, opulent wealth and dire poverty. Surrounded on three sides by water (the Atlantic, the Pacific, and the Southern oceans), South America was once an island continent. But about 3 million years ago volcanic action built the Isthmus of Panama, connecting South America to Central America.

At 6.9 million square miles (11.1 million sq km), South America ranks as the fourth largest continent, but much of the land is virtually uninhabited and completely inhospitable to human settlement.

EUROPE'S CULTURAL INFLUENCES

Three centuries of **European colonization** left its mark on the cultures of South America. Roman Catholicism, introduced by Spain, is the major religion in the region, and Spanish and Portuguese (in Brazil, the largest country) are the dominant languages. There are pockets of indigenous languages, and

French is spoken in French Guiana and Dutch in Suriname. The largest impact the Europeans had on the continent was the spread of disease, to which the native population had developed no immunity. Within a short time of the first European contact with the New World, about 80 percent of the native population succumbed to smallpox, diphtheria, measles, mumps, typhus, and other Old World diseases.

Today the vast majority of people live in cities. The rural areas, mostly rugged mountains and inaccessible rainforest, are sparsely populated. In the cities the extremes of wealth and poverty are obvious; however, an emerging middle class is bringing about rapid social and economic growth in some regions. Political volatility, enormous foreign debt, a colonial history of plundered resources, and a rapidly expanding population are some of the continent's major issues.

THE COUNTRIES OF SOUTH AMERICA

Remember those map quizzes where you had to fill in the countries? Well, South America is almost as easy to figure out as North America. Start at the top with Venezuela and go counterclockwise in a giant C to Colombia; then smaller Ecuador; long, narrow Peru; then land-locked Bolivia. Place huge Brazil inside that C-shape, stretching all the way to the Atlantic Coast. North of Brazil, along the eastern edge of Venezuela, fill in Guyana, Suriname, and French Guiana. Back on the Pacific Coast, put Chile along the southern coast and stretch out Argentina along the Atlantic Coast. You are left with small Paraguay and smaller Uruguay. Tuck them south of Brazil, with Paraguay almost on top of Uruguay (alphabetical order north to south). A+!

THE 12 INDEPENDENT NATIONS OF SOUTH AMERICA

COUNTRY	CAPITAL	AREA*	POPULATION**
Argentina	Buenos Aires	1,074	40.9
Bolivia	La Paz	424	9.8
Brazil	Brasilia	3,300	198.7
Chile	Santiago	292	16.6
Colombia	Bogota	440	45.6
Ecuador	Quito	109	14.6
Guyana	Georgetown	83	0.8
Paraguay	Asunción	157	7.0
Peru	Lima	496	29.5
Suriname	Paramaribo	63	0.5
Uruguay	Montevideo	68	3.5
Venezuela	Caracas	352	26.8

*in thousands of square miles
**in millions

In addition to the 12 independent nations of South America, there are three major territories. The **Falkland Islands** are a group of islands off the coast of Argentina, claimed by both the United Kingdom and Argentina (Argentina calls them the Malvanias). The **Galapagos Islands,** an archipelago of 13 large islands and more than 40 tiny islands, lies in the Pacific Ocean about 600 miles (960 km) west of Ecuador and is a province of Ecuador. The Galapagos are famous as the site that led **Charles Darwin** to develop his theory of evolution.

Since 1959, when Ecuador made 97 percent of the land area of Galapagos a national park, tourism has become its biggest industry. The islands were internationally recognized as a **World Heritage Site** by UNESCO in December 2001. **French Guiana** is a holdover of South America's colonial past.

> ## 🌐 GEO GEM
>
> **What's the Difference between a Rainforest and a Jungle?**
> Both are areas of dense growth and abundant moisture and heat. However, a rainforest is characterized by a high canopy and little undergrowth, while a jungle has dense undergrowth but no canopy.

Technically it is an overseas department (*département d'outre-mer,* or DOM) of France. Located on the northern Atlantic coast of South America, it borders Brazil to the east and south and Suriname to the west. Its principal industry, oddly enough, is space travel. This is the site of Europe's Spaceport, the launch facility for the European Space Agency.

HIGHLANDS AND LOWLANDS: FROM MOUNTAIN PEAKS TO RIVER BASIN

The physical geography of the South American continent is dominated by the Andes, which runs down the western edge of the continent, and the Amazon River Basin, located to the east of the Andes. Additionally, there are highlands, deserts, and grasslands.

The Andes

This massive mountain system of rugged high peaks extends from the northern end of South America all the way south to Tierra del Fuego, the archipelago off the tip of the mainland. Formed by the same plate tectonic subduction process that

THE MOTHER OF ALL GRAINS

The Andes offer little in the way of arable land, but the Incas managed to domesticate one grain. Quinoa—pronounced *KEEN-wa*—has been showing up in health-food markets and on inventive restaurant menus for the last decade or so. Although it is called a grain and looks like millet, it is not a true grain—that is, a member of the grass family. Instead, it is the seed of a plant related to the spinach family.

And what a seed it is! Quinoa has been a high-protein staple food for the people living in the Andes for at least 9,000 years. This plant is one of the few food crops that can survive in such high altitudes (10,000 to 20,000 feet/3,050 to 6,100 m above sea level), withstanding the frost, intense sun, and recurring drought that characterizes the Andean climate. Once American food processors learned to soak quinoa in an alkaline solution to wash off the bitter coating that protects the seeds from birds, quinoa gained attention in U.S. markets. Today it is mainly imported from Bolivia, Peru, and Chile, although small amounts are grown in the United States and Canadian Rockies.

formed the Rockies in North America, the Andes are fold mountains. They rise to 22,835 feet (6,960 m) above sea level at the peak of Aconcagua in Argentina and extend for almost 4,500 miles (7,242 km).

The Amazon and most of the other major rivers on the continent originate in the Andes, which is where the continental divide is located. The Andes are also home to some of the planet's largest volcanoes, and in the far south along the coast of Chile, large glaciers are common.

Latitude plays a defining role in the climates of this lengthy mountain range. In the northern region it is warmer and wetter because those mountains are closest to the equator. Still, the high mountains are snowcapped—like Mount Cotopaxi in Ecuador, which is just 30 miles (48 km) from the equator. The region is humid and rainy, and the vegetation is lush, as hikers on the Inca Trail to Machu Picchu readily find. To the east lies the vast rainforest of the **Amazon Basin.** In the Central Andes the western side is extremely dry and includes the **Atacama Desert** in northern Chile. In some locations in the desert, no rain has been recorded in the last 400 years. The eastern portion of the central Andes is much wetter. In the southern region the mountains are relatively close to the Antarctic, and the climate is far colder. The western side of the Andes tends to be wet, while the eastern plains of Argentina are in a rain shadow and are very dry. Many of the peaks in the Andes receive heavy snowfall and contain glaciers.

THE COLOMBIAN EXCHANGE

Centuries of isolation caused by the breakup of the supercontinent Pangaea resulted in the evolution of completely different food crops in the Old and New World. Once European explorers came to the New World, there was a fairly rapid transfer of plants and animals—and disease—between the Old World and the New.

The Americas provided corn, potatoes, tomatoes, peppers, pumpkins, squash, pineapples, cacao beans (for chocolate), sweet potatoes, and turkeys. Tobacco, an American product, was also sent off to Europe. From Europe, the Americas were introduced to wheat, cattle, pigs, and sheep, as well as gunpowder and horses.

African products introduced to the Americas included items that originated in Asia and were brought to the West by European traders and African slaves. These items included onions, citrus fruits, bananas, coffee beans, olives, grapes, rice, and sugarcane.

Amazon Basin

The world's **largest tropical rainforest,** at 2.5 million square miles (4.02 million sq km), the Amazon Basin is roughly the size of 48 contiguous states of mainland United States. It covers about one third of the continent, with nearly 60 percent of it within Brazil. Another 13 percent lies within the borders of Peru; smaller areas are in Colombia, Venezuela, Ecuador, Bolivia, Guyana, Suriname, and French Guiana.

The Amazon is the wettest of the world's rainforests. Heavy rains drench much of the densely forested lowlands throughout the year, but especially between January and June. The vegetation of the rainforest includes a variety of trees, including tropical hardwoods, palms, tree ferns, and bamboos. The trees grow so close together that their crowns form a dense canopy.

UP IN THE CLOUDS

Where rainforests meet mountains, cloud forests happen. These highland tropical forests cover the slopes of the Andean mountains from about 3,000 feet (900 m) to about 8,000 feet (2500 m). A cloud forest is cooler than a tropical rainforest and is covered by an almost constant mist—or low-lying cloud—throughout the year.

The foliage harbors a wide diversity of epiphytes ("air plants" or plants whose roots are not in the soil), and tree trunks are almost always covered with mosses, bromeliads, ferns, lichens, and other plants. Together they function as a huge net to capture moisture. As moisture-laden winds are forced up the mountains, the air cools as it rises in altitude, and moisture is squeezed out to form the water droplets that make up the almost ever-present clouds. One of the defining features of a cloud forest (as opposed to a rainforest) is that in a cloud forest most of the moisture comes from horizontal mists, and a lesser amount is received as rain (vertical drops).

The canopy may soar up to 130 feet (40 m) and is so impenetrable that sunlight seldom reaches the forest floor.

Rainforests are notable for sustaining vast numbers of different plant and animal species, but the **biodiversity** of the Amazon Basin is unparalleled, with more species of plants and animals per square mile than anywhere else on the planet. One in 10 known species in the world live in the Amazon Rainforest, including 1 in 5 bird species. The region is home to about 2.5 million insect species, at least 40,000 species of plants, 3,000 species of fish, 400 species of mammals, 400 species of amphibians, and 400 species of reptiles. The biodiversity of the tropical rainforest is so immense that less than 1 percent of its millions of species have been studied by scientists for their active constituents and their possible uses.

 **GEO GEM**

Highest City in the World
Denver is known as the mile-high city in the United States because of its elevation above sea level: 5,280 feet (1,609 m). La Rinconada in Peru is the highest city in the world, with an elevation of 16,728 feet (5,098 m). That makes it the 3-mile-high city.

More Lowlands and Highlands

Like all continents, South America features a variety of landforms.

Guiana Highlands. In north-central South America, a rolling plateau crossed by low mountain ranges.

Los Llanos. Think grassy plains, sun-parched during the dry season, inundated and partially flooded during the rainy season. This land, really the Orinoco River basin, is north of the Amazon Rainforest, stretching across much of Venezuela and Colombia and extending to the shores of the Caribbean.

Pantanal. The world's largest wetland of any kind, this tropical wetland is 80 percent under water during the rainy season. It lies mostly within Brazil but extends into portions of Bolivia and Paraguay, sprawling over an area estimated at between 54,000 and 75,000 square miles (140,000 to 195,000 sq km). The name comes from the Portuguese word *pântano,* meaning wetland or marsh.

Brazilian Highlands. Occupying a large part of eastern South America is the Brazilian Highlands, a rolling, hilly plateau 1,000 to 3,000 feet (300 to 900 m) above sea level.

Altiplano. Spanish for high plain, the Altiplano is located in west-central South America, where the Andes are at their widest. It is the most extensive area of high plateau on Earth outside of Tibet. **Lake Titicaca,** the cradle of the Incan civilization, and the largest lake in South America, is its best-known geographical feature.

Atacama Desert. One of the driest spots on the planet, the Atacama Desert lies southwest of the Altiplano in the rain shadow of the Andes.

GEO GEM

Highest Lake

At an elevation of 12,500 feet (3810 m), Lake Titicaca is the highest navigable lake in the world. It borders both Peru and Bolivia.

Gran Chaco. An extensive lowland plain divided among Paraguay, Bolivia, and Argentina. Gran Chaco boasts some of the highest temperatures in South America.

Pampas. Merging with the Gran Chaco to the

THE LAND OF FOUR QUARTERS

The great Incan Empire was short-lived, from 1428 to 1533, but it was a marvel of human adaptation to circumstances dictated by geography.

The Incas controlled an empire in the Central Andes in an area that stretched from Colombia to Chile, some 2,500 miles (4,023 km). Cuzco was the capital city. Daily life was spent at altitudes up to 15,000 feet (4,572 m), and ritual life extended up to 22,057 feet (6,723 m) to Llullaillaco in Chile, the highest Inca sacrificial site known today. The landscape was one of steep mountains, fertile valleys, desert, and raging rivers, and the Inca's success was a result of their ability to generate food surpluses.

By building terraces and irrigation systems, the Incas became successful farmers. With food supplies guaranteed, the empire was able to expand. Building a network of roads and bridges enabled the Incas to unify their territory, allowing for the movement of soldiers, tributes, and goods. In order to build these roads and their sacrificial platforms, loads of soil, rock, and grass had to be hauled up the mountains to incomprehensible heights—by people who didn't use the wheel or horses. One road ran almost the entire length of the South American Pacific Coast! The Incas paved their highland roads with flat stones and built stone walls to prevent travelers from falling off cliffs.

The Incas divided their empire into four quarters for efficient administration. They developed and imposed on others a common language known as Quecha. At its peak, Incan society had more than 6 million people.

Their skilled metalwork—particularly in gold and silver—was what attracted the Spanish explorers, eventually leading to the colonization of the entire continent.

north, the Argentine Pampas is a flat and highly fertile plains region famous for its *gauchos* (cowboys) and cattle ranches. The climate in the pampas is humid and warm.

Patagonia. The narrow southern end of the continent, east of the Andes, is a harsh semiarid plateau characterized by extremely high winds and scanty vegetation.

THE AMAZING AMAZON

North Americans talk about "the mighty Mississippi," but mighty doesn't even begin to describe the Amazon River, which carries the volume of water of 10 Mississippis, or more than two thirds of all the fresh water found on Earth.

THE GREAT AMERICAN INTERCHANGE

After the Isthmus of Panama was formed for some 3 million years, the movement of plants and animals as a result of this new land bridge was dubbed the Great American Interchange. Most of the record is contained in fossilized remains, and many of the traveling flora and fauna didn't find success in their new habitats. Animals that made the journey from South America to North America successfully are giant ground sloths, armadillos, opossums, and porcupines. When you think about it, their "foreign" origins aren't surprising, since they are surely the oddest-looking animals in all of North America.

Traveling south were mammoths, mastodons, tapirs, peccaries, rabbits, deer, bear, squirrels, hamsters, horses, and camels, largely replacing the native mammal community. The introduction of northern predators into South America was particularly devastating. Between competition and predation, much of the local fauna that had survived for millions of years went extinct within a relatively short period of time.

Combined with its 1,100 tributaries, the Amazon carries the greatest volume of water of any river in the world.

At a length of 6,500 miles (10,460 km), the Amazon River is not the longest river in the world; that distinction goes to the Nile. The river starts as a glacial stream high in the Andes and flows more than 4,000 miles (6,436 km) across the South American continent until it becomes some 1 to 6 miles (1.6 to 10 km) across during the dry season and some 30 miles (48 km) or more across during the wet season. The force of the current, from sheer water volume alone—and the fact that saltwater is heavier than fresh water—causes the river water to continue flowing about 125 miles (201 km) out to sea before fully mixing with Atlantic saltwater.

GEO GEM

Farthest from Earth's Center

The farthest point on the Earth's crust from the Earth's center is Mount Chimborazo in the Ecuadorean Andes (3,929 miles/6,323 km).

LIFE IN THE CITIES

Asiatic hunters and gatherers are thought to have been the first settlers, probably arriving less than 12,000 years ago. They may have arrived via the ocean or via the Bering Strait land bridge that also brought people to North America.

Prior to the arrival of the Europeans in the 1500s, the Incan Empire achieved notable feats of agriculture and engineering in the central Andes. Outside the Incan territory, populations of semi-nomadic tribes subsisted on hunting, fishing, gathering, and migrant agriculture. Then the Europeans arrived, searching for gold and later settling in the region.

The population today—almost 400 million people, of which about half live in Brazil—is a mix of Amerindians,

Europeans, and Africans, with mestizos (people of Amerindian and European ancestry), zambos (people of Amerindian and African ancestry), and mulattos or creoles (of European and African descent). There are also sizeable communities of Middle Easterners, East Asians, and Japanese. Although South America's population is relatively small—some 5.6 percent of the world's total—it is growing rapidly.

Since the 1970s, urbanization has been rapid. Strikingly, the majority of the population is found near the edges of the continent, especially along the eastern coast and in the mountain valleys of the west. Outside the cities the population density of the continent is very low, with vast portions of the interior virtually uninhabited. Most of the people live within 200 miles (320 km) of the coast, and only in a few places, such as the Paraná River Valley of Argentina, have densely settled areas extended any great distance into the interior.

With the exception of Quito (capital of Ecuador) and Brasilia (capital of Brazil), the largest cities in South America are also the nations' capitals. These cities also function as the economic, cultural, and political centers of the countries. **São Paulo,** Brazil, with a population of nearly 18,850,000, is the largest city of South America and the seventh largest in the world. With all the urban migration, squatter settlements have multiplied around urban areas, and unemployment is widespread.

NATURAL RESOURCES

One day a Spanish ship bumped into a small Incan reed boat carrying a cargo of silver and gold. That chance encounter confirmed the rumors the Spanish had heard—that the lands south of the Mayans was the land of gold. Although **gold and silver** are found—and mined—on the continent, the land was not—and is not—El Dorado, the mythical land of gold. South

America has one eighth of the world's total deposits of **iron** and one fourth of its **copper** reserves. **Bauxite** reserves are found in Brazil, Guyana, Suriname, and Venezuela.

GEO GEM

Name Game

Guyana was formerly known as British Guiana. Suriname was formerly known as Dutch Guiana.

Liquid, or black, gold is another story. Venezuela consistently ranks as one of the top suppliers of U.S. oil imports and is among the top ten **crude oil** producers in the world. Ecuador is another major producer of crude oil. Colombia is an important petroleum and coal producer, although political unrest has led to decreased exports in recent years. There are also petroleum reserves in Colombia, Argentina, Chile, and Peru.

Given the geography of the region, it is not surprising that less than one tenth of the land is arable. Crops include corn, wheat, rice, fruits, sugar, and coffee. Trade in illegal narcotics (mostly for export) is a major source of revenue in some countries. About one fourth of the land is suitable for grazing cattle. About half the land is covered by forest, mainly the enormous but steadily diminishing rainforest of the Amazon Basin.

Chapter 5

Asia

Did you learn in school that Asia is a continent? Well, it isn't. (If you remember, we defined a continent as a large landmass in chapter 1.) Asia is just the central and eastern part of the continent of Eurasia—what you get when you subtract the European peninsula from the continent.

The boundaries between Asia and Europe are a little vague, in part because the country of Russia stretches over the boundaries. Generally, the western boundary of Asia is defined as the Ural Mountains, the Bosporus Strait, and the Black Sea. The Isthmus of Suez is the place where Asia ends and Africa begins.

LAND OF THE LARGE

Called the **largest continent** on Earth, in terms of both area (17.2 million square miles/27.4 million sq km) and population (4 billion), Asia also boasts the world's **largest country**—the Russian Federation—and three of the four **most populous**:

China, India, and Indonesia. Thus, Asia accounts for more than 60 percent of the world population. Asia also includes thousands of nearby islands in the Indian and Pacific oceans; Indonesia with more than 17,000 islands is the **largest archipelago** in the world.

THE CHINA GIANT

China looms large over Asia—over the whole globe, really. It is both an ancient civilization whose roots can be traced back 8,000 to 10,000 years and a modern nation that was created in 1949 as the People's Republic of China. Recently, China emerged as a significant world economic power.

Population. The People's Republic of China is the third largest country in the world in terms of area, but it is the largest in terms of population: 1.2 billion. About 74 percent of the population is rural, primarily engaged in agriculture. The ethnic group known as Han Chinese accounts for about 92 percent of the total population; there are 55 different minority groups, including Buddhist Tibetans and Islamic Uyghurs.

Terrain. Think of the land as a three-step staircase. The first and lowest step is the eastern third of the country, and

(continued on page 86)

THE NATIONS OF ASIA

COUNTRY	CAPITAL	AREA*	POPULATION**
Afghanistan	Kabul	252	33.6
Armenia	Yerevan	12	3.0
Azerbaijan	Baku	33	8.2
Bahrain	Manama	0.3	0.7
Bangladesh	Dhaka	56	56.1
Bhutan	Thimphu	18	0.7
Brunei Darussalam	Bandar Seri Begawan	2	0.4
Cambodia	Phnom Penh	70	14.5
China	Beijing	3,696	1,338.6
Georgia	Tbilisi	27	4.6
India	New Delhi	1,269	1,166.1
Indonesia	Jakarta	735	240.3
Iran	Tehran	631	66.4
Iraq	Baghdad	169	28.9
Israel	Jerusalem	8	7.2
Japan	Tokyo	146	127.1
Jordan	Amman	34	6.3
Kazakhstan	Astana	1,049	15.4
Kuwait	Kuwait City	7	2.7

COUNTRY	CAPITAL	AREA*	POPULATION**
Kyrgyzstan	Bishkek	77	5.4
Laos	Vientiane	91	6.8
Lebanon	Beirut	4	4.0
Malaysia	Kuala Lumpur	127	25.7
Maldives	Malé	0.1	0.4
Mongolia	Ulan Bator	605	3.0
Myanmar	Naypyidaw	261	48.1
Nepal	Kathmandu	57	28.6
North Korea	Pyongyang	47	22.7
Oman	Muscat	82	3.4
Pakistan	Islamabad	307	176.2
Philippines	Manila	116	98.0
Qatar	Doha	4	0.8
Russian Federation	Moscow	6,593	140.0
Saudi Arabia	Riyadh	830	28.7
Singapore	Singapore	0.2	4.7
South Korea	Seoul	38	48.5
Sri Lanka	Colombo	25	21.3
Syria	Damascus	71	20.2

THE NATIONS OF ASIA *(continued)*

COUNTRY	CAPITAL	AREA*	POPULATION**
Tajikistan	Dushanbe	55	7.3
Thailand	Bangkok	198	65.9
East Timor	Dili	6	1.1
Turkmenistan	Ashgabat	188	4.9
United Arab Emirates	Abu Dhabi	32	4.8
Uzbekistan	Tashkent	173	27.6
Vietnam	Hanoi	128	97.0
Yemen	Sana'a	204	23.6

*in thousands of square miles
**in millions

the elevation climbs from there, moving west. Plains and lowlands are the central second step, while mountains and high plateaus (the third step) are found in the west.

Rivers. Two great rivers dominate the landscape and history of China. The **Yangtze River** in the south, at 3,925 miles (6,300 km) in length, is the longest in China and the third longest in the world. It originates in the glaciers of Tibet, cuts through limestone gorges in dramatic shifts in elevation, and flows into the East China Sea in Shanghai. Several large cities, including Shanghai, Nanjing, Wuhan, and Chongqing, lie in the river's rich agricultural basin—the granary of China. A very large percentage of China's population lives in the eastern portion of the basin. For thousands of years, the Yangtze has provided transportation and water for manufacturing, irrigation, and household uses. The Three Gorges Dam, the world's largest hydropower plant, is located on the Yangtze. Flooding, pollution, and destruction of wetlands are all threats facing the river and its basin.

China's **"cradle of civilization"** lies along the **Yellow River,** or Huang He, the second longest river in China. At 3,395 miles (5,464 km) long, it begins in the Tibetan Plateau and winds through the northern part of China, where it passes through a loess plateau. This is where it picks up

 **GEO GEM**

The Formation of Land Bridges

Everyone knows that a land bridge between Siberia and Alaska allowed early man to cross from Asia into North America. But how did the land bridge form?

During the last Ice Age, the ice sheets were so massive and took up so much water that global sea levels fell by about 400 feet (120 m), exposing continental shelves. Many islands became connected with the continents through dry land. This was the case between the Siberia and Alaska, and also between the British Isles and Europe, Taiwan and China, and the Indonesian islands and Asia.

a yellowish sediment—hence, the name. Loess soils are made from deposits left by wind over centuries; it is extremely fertile and easy to farm, but it erodes very easily. As the river makes its way to the sea, it carries tons of silt, continually raising the riverbed, which is one reason the Yellow River changes course and floods frequently. And because it flows through heavily populated areas, death tolls from flooding have been huge. Some people drown initially, while others die from the spread of diseases and famine. A flood in 1887 killed 2 million people. Today the Yellow River is a dying river, with poorly conceived dams diverting the flow, industrial pollution tainting the water, and drought and desertification in its basin severely reducing its flow.

Climate. In a country so vast, with so many changes in both latitude and elevation, there are many climate zones. In terms of temperature, the nation can be divided from north to south into different zones: cold-temperate, temperate, warm-temperate, subtropical, tropical, and equatorial. In terms of moisture, it can be divided from northwest to southeast into an arid zone (31 percent of the land), a semi-arid zone (22 percent of the land), semi-humid zone (15 percent of the land), and humid zone (32 percent of the land).

There are two distinct dry and wet **monsoon seasons,** with the rainy season also being the hot season. In the winter, northern winds coming from the high latitudes are cold and dry; in summer, southern winds from the sea at lower latitudes are warm and moist. In the south, rain is abundant and temperatures are relatively high.

Arable Land. With only 7 percent of the world's arable land, huge China is land poor. The arable land is found primarily in the southeast, where China produces more than one quarter of the global rice harvest. Extensive areas of western China are relatively uninhabited and inhospitable; the **Gobi Desert** makes up about 30 percent of China's land.

THE NONSTATE OF TAIWAN

The large island of Taiwan, formerly known as Formosa, off the shore of mainland China is claimed by the People's Republic of China but has a government that is neither under China's control nor independent. Taiwan has a strong economy and is a major supplier of the world's computer chips and LCD panels.

THE EXPANDING DESERT

The most extreme environment in China is found in the **Gobi Desert,** a barren badland of gravel plains and rocky outcroppings. Covering much of the southern part of Mongolia, this high-altitude "cold" desert has temperatures ranging from 122°F (50°C) in the summer to −40°F (−40°C) in winter. On average, less than 4 inches (10 cm) of precipitation falls in a year. A portion of the Gobi is desert steppe rangeland with just enough vegetation to support camels, but the Gobi also includes areas of no vegetation whatsoever. Overgrazing, soil erosion from wind, and mining activities have all been identified as environmental problems in the region. Desert accounts for about one quarter of China's land, and this desert is expanding at an alarming rate, edging ever closer to the capital city of Beijing with mighty dust storms.

Natural Resources. The country is rich in mineral reserves and is one of the largest producers of antimony, zinc, and tungsten. China also has reserves of coal, iron ore, gold, copper, magnetite, petroleum, aluminum, natural gas, mercury, tin, lead, manganese, molybdenum, vanadium, and uranium. It has considerable hydropower available to it.

TIBET: CULTURE AND GEOGRAPHIC ISOLATION

On a treeless plateau above 13,000 feet (4,000 m) in elevation, surrounded by mountains, reside the people of Tibet. They lived in relative isolation for centuries, creating a distinctive culture, influenced by but distinctly different from India to the west and China to the east. This isolation led to a very strong cultural identity based on common language and religion. The people of Tibet are Buddhist and deeply religious, and the monasteries of Tibet form the basis of the education

🌐 GEO GEM

Wettest Place in the World

Cherrapunji, India, prides itself on being the wettest place on Earth, with a record year of 905 inches (30 m) between August 1860 and July 1861. When you consider that 1 inch (2.5 cm) of rain means that 4 gallons (15 L) of water falls on each square yard (0.8 sq m), you begin to see the problem.

system and economy of the region.

Winter in Tibet lasts from October until May or June. Due to its high altitude, Tibet's seasonal variation in temperature is limited, but daily temperature variation can be extreme. For example, the temperature in Lhasa can range as much as -2°F to 85°F (-19°C to 30°C) in a single day. Tibet has two seasons: the dry season (from October to April) and the rainy season (from May to September). About 18 inches (46 cm) of precipitation fall each year.

Outside of Tibetan cities the indigenous population is made up of nomads, farmers (barley and root vegetables are primary crops), and forest dwellers. The nomads rely on grazing animals—yaks, sheep, and goats.

Tibet closed its borders to foreigners in 1792, a reaction against the British in India. This kept the British out until 1903, when Great Britain took Tibet by force in order to establish an overland trade route with China. In 1906 the British and Chinese signed a peace treaty, and Great Britain "gave" Tibet to the Chinese. (The Chinese signed the treaty, not the Tibetans, claiming that Tibet had been part of China since the thirteenth century). Five years later Tibet expelled the Chinese and declared independence. That independence lasted until 1950, when China invaded Tibet. Since 1965 China has administered Tibet as the "Autonomous Region of Tibet" (Xizang), meanwhile encouraging ethnic Han Chinese to relocate to Tibet, sweetening the deal with development money and a high-altitude railroad. The Chinese government has a strategic interest in maintaining access to Tibet's vast reserves of copper, chromium, iron, lead, zinc, and most important, fresh water.

EAST ASIA: PLATE TECTONICS AT WORK

East Asia is dominated by China, but the area also includes the island nation of **Japan** and **North and South Korea** on the Korean Peninsula.

Tectonic plate action played no small role in the formation of this region. When the Indo-Australian Plate pushed beneath the Eurasian Plate, besides adding the subcontinent of India and lifting the massive Himalayan Mountains, the twisting movement of the Philippine Plate caused a portion of eastern Asia to sink, creating the shallow Yellow Sea and the East China Sea. As the Pacific Plate and the large North American Plate pressed north and west along the Pacific Rim, it forced areas of eastern Asia to tilt westward, lifting the Japanese archipelago from the waters of the Pacific. North of these islands, near the eastern edge of the Asian continent, the Earth's crust buckled, thrusting its granite foundation upward to create the Korean peninsula, a jagged landmass that stretches nearly 600 miles (966 km) southward from the Asian continent. Over time many of the smaller mountains in this region disappeared beneath the waters of the Yellow Sea, creating thousands of small islands off Korea's south and west coasts.

NAPOLEON ON CHINA

About two centuries ago Napoleon Bonaparte is said to have pointed to China on a globe and stated, "Here lies a sleeping giant. Let her sleep, for when she wakes, she will shake the world."

🌍 GEO GEM

River in Reverse

The Tonle Sap River in Cambodia reverses direction every year. Normally, the Tonle Sap flows south, draining into Mekong River. Then the monsoons come, pouring so much water into the Mekong River that it briefly forces the Tonle Sap River to flow backward, swelling the Tonle Sap Lake in western Cambodia to more than five times its normal size. The result of this unusual situation is an extremely productive fishery.

Terrain. Mountains dominate the Korean Peninsula and Japan, leaving only about 15 percent of land suitable for agriculture.

Climate. The climate of East Asia is temperate, with cold winters and hot summers. Most of the rainfall occurs during the summer, allowing intensive agriculture, with two and sometimes three crop cycles per year. In the winter, cold winds from the northern Asian continent blow east over the Sea of Japan, dumping deep, heavy snow on the northwestern coast, Japan's "snow country."

Earthquakes and Volcanoes. Japan lies on the cusp of a junction among the Pacific, Philippine, and Eurasian plates. Earthquakes are frequent in Japan, and occasionally they do serious damage.

The mountains of Japan include about 200 active volcanoes, which is 10 percent of the world's most active. **Mount Fuji** (elevation 12,388 feet/3776 m) is Japan's tallest and most famous mountain; it is a dormant (sleeping but not extinct) volcano that last erupted in 1707. Korea has dealt with many restless earthquakes and volcanoes.

Mongolia and the "Stans"

Although there is no strict definition of Central Asia, it is usually thought to include **Mongolia** and the five republics of the former Soviet Union: **Kazakhstan, Kyrgyzstan, Tajikistan, Turkmenistan,** and **Uzbekistan.** "Stan" is Persian for "place of." (Afghanistan, Pakistan, Kashmir, and at times

---

THE SILK ROAD AND THE BOOK

Before the age of railroads and airplanes, Europe, China, South Asia, and the Middle East connected economically, politically, and culturally via overland trade routes through Central Asia, most notably via the Silk Road. Among the many treasures of the East that arrived in Europe that way, papermaking, printing, gunpowder, the compass, and silk-making were perhaps the most important.

Marco Polo was one of the most famous merchants who traveled the Silk Road. His impact was lasting because he had the "leisure" to dictate stories of his travels to a cellmate during an unfortunate period of imprisonment. *The Travels of Marco Polo* by Rustichello da Pisa relates Polo's travels throughout Asia between 1271 and 1291.

It is said that Christopher Columbus's decision to reach the Far East was heavily influenced by his reading of the book. The book also influenced the cartographers of the fifteenth century, who used the names of places as related by Polo. Giving Polo credit for inspiring Columbus's quest to find an oceanic route to the East is far more likely than giving Polo credit for bringing pasta to Italy. Most food historians think that pasta was developed separately in the East and West. Meanwhile, Christopher Columbus's heavily annotated copy of *The Travels of Marco Polo* can be seen at the Colombian Library in Seville, Spain.

parts of western China and southern Siberia in Russia are sometimes, but not always, considered part of Central Asia. Also, it is important to keep in mind that there are two Mongolias: the independent nation of Mongolia and the Inner Mongolia Autonomous Region in China. Here we are talking about the independent nation.)

Geographically, this is the **Eurasian Steppes.** Although the region includes mountains, forests, and desert, it is dominated by treeless, grassy steppes, land that is too dry and rugged for farming. It has an extreme continental climate with long, cold winters and short summers, during which most of its annual precipitation (about 18 inches/46 cm) falls. Historically, few major cities developed in the region; instead, the area was dominated by nomadic horse people. Today a majority of the people still earn a living by herding livestock.

Those steppe horsemen were famed warriors, limited only by the inability to form alliances. But every once in a while, great leaders—such as Attila the Hun and Genghis Khan—organized several tribes into a relentless army. Then sovereigns were toppled and maps redrawn.

Once the use of firearms became widespread in the sixteenth century, the dominance of the warring nomadic horsemen was over. Russia, China, and other powers captured the bulk of Central Asia by the end of the nineteenth century.

🌏 GEO GEM

The Highs, the Lows

Asia has the world's highest peak, Mount Everest; the highest plateau, the Tibet Plateau; the lowest depression, the Dead Sea; the deepest lake, Lake Baikal; the largest lake, the Caspian Sea (yes, it really is a lake); the largest peninsula, the Arabian Peninsula; and the largest archipelago, the Marx and Lenin islands.

After the Russian Revolution the Central Asian regions were incorporated into the Soviet Union, except for Mongolia, which became an independent Soviet satellite.

Under the Soviets the population of the region increased significantly—and rarely by choice. There was much industrialization and construction of infrastructure. At the same time, the Soviets suppressed local cultures

 **GEO GEM**

Record Holder
Lake Baikal is the oldest freshwater lake on Earth, formed between 20 and 25 million years ago as a rift valley between two separating tectonic plates. The area around the lake is geologically active, with some 2,000 tremors recorded annually. The lake is also the deepest in the world and holds a volume of water equivalent to all five of America's Great Lakes.

and left a lasting legacy of ethnic tensions and environmental problems. With the collapse of the Soviet Union, the five "Stans" and Mongolia gained independence. The modern country of Mongolia, however, represents only part of the Mongols' historical homeland; more ethnic Mongolians live in the Inner Mongolia Autonomous Region in the People's Republic of China than in Mongolia.

RICE PADDIES AND VOLCANOES: SOUTHEAST ASIA

Varied geography, a stormy history, and many rich cultures are all apt descriptions of Southeast Asia. Spreading over 1.7 million square miles (4.5 million sq km), Southeast Asia is bounded on the west by India, the north by China, and on the east by the Pacific Ocean. Most of the region falls within the humid equatorial tropics, with the seasonal heavy rains of a monsoon climate. In mountainous regions high altitudes result in more moderate temperatures and drier landscapes. Although threatened by logging, the rainforest is the second largest on Earth.

The region divides up neatly into two distinctive geographic and cultural zones: mainland Southeast Asia, also known as Indochina, and maritime Southeast Asia, or the Malay Archipelago. Historically, the inland states have developed rice-based agricultural economies, while the maritime states focused on trading.

THE WALLACE LINE

In the mid-1800s Alfred Russel Wallace—biologist, anthropologist, and explorer-adventurer—was studying the flora and fauna of the Malay Archipelago. He was struck by the sudden difference in bird families he encountered when he sailed some 20 miles (32 km) east of the island of Bali and landed on the island of Lombok. On Bali he observed birds that were clearly related to those of the larger islands of Java and Sumatra and mainland Malaysia. On Lombok the birds were clearly related to those of New Guinea and Australia. He marked the channel between Bali and Lombok as the divide between two great zoogeographic regions and suggested that the land might have been joined at some point in history.

His discovery was the start of a field of inquiry known as **biogeography,** which looks at the distributions of species in terms of both regional differences and historical changes in the environment. It turns out that the Wallace Line actually marks the edge of the Asian continental shelf, and plate tectonics explains the distribution of the species he studied.

It seems that some of the islands on each of the plates were once connected to each other and to the mainland by land bridges. Animals could freely migrate among them, though no such bridge existed between the two plates.

Rice is the chief crop of the region; rubber, tea, spices, and coconuts are also important. The region has a great variety of minerals and produces most of the world's tin.

The culture and life-styles of the people are diverse. Most people live

GEO GEM

Japan: An Archipelago

Japan consists of four principal islands: Hokkaido, Honshu, Shikoku, and Kyushu and more than 3,000 adjacent islands and islets, including Okinawa.

in small agrarian settlements, but there are also large cities such as Jakarta, Bangkok, and Singapore. Ethnicity and languages throughout the region vary greatly, as do religious beliefs and historical experiences.

The Mainland

The land is mountainous, with large river systems. Population on the peninsula is unevenly distributed, with the larger cities clinging to the coastline.

Vietnam. Vietnam has a 2,000-year history of foreign intervention, most famously in a conflict the Vietnamese call the American War. Unlike the other Southeast Asia nations, Vietnam has been more influenced by Chinese culture than by Indian. The land is dominated by two fertile river delta regions— the Mekong and the Red (Hong) River, separated by rugged, mountainous terrain and the central Annamese Highlands.

Laos. One of the poorest nations of the world, landlocked Lao People's Democratic Republic lies north of Cambodia, between the Mekong River and the Annamese Highlands. Most of the population survives with fishing and subsistence farming. The country was not opened up to tourism until 1989.

Cambodia. The Kingdom of Cambodia is a country of low plains lying between Thailand and Vietnam. About 20 percent of the land is arable and intensively farmed. The country has a long history of warfare and political instability; its economy is underdeveloped and dependent on foreign aid.

Thailand. The name means "Free Land," and Thailand is the only nation in the region never conquered by a Western power. Much of the land is covered by forested highlands—tropical rainforests, deciduous forests, and coniferous pine forests. A central lowland plain, drained by the river Chao Phraya, is rich and fertile. Thailand is the fifth largest exporter of rice in the world, and more than half the population is involved in agriculture. Tourism contributes significantly to the economy.

Myanmar. The Union of Myanmar, formerly called Burma, is a multiethnic country that lies largely between China and India. Geographically isolated by mountain ranges running north to south, Myanmar's military dictatorship oversees an agricultural nation with a poorly developed industrial sector. Until recently, foreign investment and tourism were severely restricted.

🌐 GEO GEM

Land Grab

The Spratly Islands, a small chain of islands and reefs off the coast of Vietnam in the South China Sea, are claimed by Brunei, China, Malaysia, Taiwan, Vietnam, and the Philippines. Why do they want it? The islands are surrounded by rich fishing grounds and likely contain reserves of underwater oil and cobalt.

The Malay Archipelago

Spreading across the tip of the mainland peninsula and bordered

KRAKATAU: THE VOLCANO
HEARD ROUND THE WORLD

In August 1883 Krakatau erupted and killed somewhere between 40,000 and 120,000 people (estimates vary wildly), mostly through resulting tsunamis. The eruption destroyed more than 70 percent of the island. The force of the eruption discharged the energy equivalent of 13,000 nuclear bombs similar to the size and strength of Little Boy, which was dropped on Hiroshima during World War II.

The eruption was heard at least 3,000 miles (4,828 km) away—perhaps the loudest sound in human history. At close range the sound was literally deafening. The average global temperature fell by 2°F (1.2°C) in the year following the eruption, and spectacular sunsets were recorded around the world.

In 1930 another volcanic island, Anak Krakatau, which translates as Krakatoa's Child, emerged from the seabed. This young volcano grows an estimated 16 feet (5 m) each year and became very active in 2010.

by the Indian Ocean, the South China Sea, and Pacific Ocean, the Malay Archipelago is made up of **Brunei, East Malaysia, East Timor, Indonesia, the Philippines,** and **Singapore.** It is the **largest archipelago** in the world, covering more than 750,000 square miles (1,950,000 sq km) and consisting of 25,000 islands. The Philippines account for more than 7,000 islands, and Indonesia accounts for another 17,000 to 18,000 islands. Included in the island count are numerous uninhabited volcanic and coral islands. Compared to the mainland country, these island countries are geographically smaller, and the populations are also smaller, with the exception of Indonesia.

Brunei. The tiny State of Brunei Darussalem on the northwest coast of the island of Borneo has a population of under half a million and boasts one of the highest per capita incomes in Asia. The Sultan of Brunei is believed to be one of the richest men in the world, thanks to vast oil and natural-gas deposits found on- and offshore.

Malaysia. Malaysia is both a peninsula and an island nation. It shares the Malay Peninsula with Thailand, and the large island of Borneo to the east with Indonesia and Brunei. The islands of Malaysia have fertile volcanic soils and large regions of tropical rainforests, with an enormous diversity in the native plant and wildlife. Malaysia exports rubber and tin.

Singapore. An island off the tip of the Malay Peninsula, the Republic of Singapore was once upon a time covered by dense rainforest. Today it is an urban area with one of the world's highest population densities (16,732 people per square mile). Singapore is a financial center and is known as the Switzerland of Southeast Asia. Its deepwater harbor, basically the small country's only natural resource, serves as a base for fleets engaged in offshore drilling in the region. Singapore must import all its food and drinking water.

🌎 GEO GEM

What in the World Is Asia Minor?

In the days when the Middle East was the Near East, there was another term kicking around: Asia Minor. Today Asia Minor is most likely referred to as Anatolia: the westernmost protrusion of Asia, which is occupied by Turkey.

The region was home to many civilizations throughout history, including the Hittites, Phrygians, Lydians, Persians, Greeks, Assyrians, Armenians, Romans, Byzantines, Anatolian Seljuks, and Ottomans, making Anatolia an archaeologist's paradise.

Indonesia. The people of the Republic of Indonesia are a mixture of more than 100 ethnic groups, speak about 300 languages, and live on 5 major islands and about 30 groups of smaller islands. Java is home to 17 of Indonesia's 100 active volcanoes. A total of 327

GEO GEM

Coral Reefs
The shallow waters of the Southeast Asian coral reefs have the highest levels of biodiversity of any of the world's marine ecosystems.

volcanoes stretch across Indonesia. In late December, 2004, a major tsunami took nearly 127,000 lives, left more than 93,000 people missing and displaced about 441,000, and destroyed almost $5 billion worth of property.

Oil and gas are Indonesia's main exports. Indonesia is a member of OPEC (Organization of Petroleum Exporting Countries).

East Timor. The Portuguese colonized the small island of Timor in the sixteenth century, because they were initially attracted to the sandalwood trees. It remained a Portuguese territory until 1975, when it was invaded by Indonesia. After a bloody war for independence, the Democratic Republic of Timor-Leste, the eastern portion of the island, was recognized as a sovereign nation in 2002. It is considered one of the poorest nations in the world, and it is the only Asian nation to lie entirely within the Southern Hemisphere.

The Philippines. The Republic of the Philippines is a melting pot, showing cultural influences from the Malays and Chinese who settled there, as well as Spanish and American occupiers. Much of the land is covered with tropical forest, yielding bamboo and lumber. The fertile volcanic soil produces crops of rice, corn, coconut, and sugarcane. Marine life is abundant.

THE MAJESTIC HIMALAYAS

The **highest mountain range** in the world, the Himalayas stretch about 1,860 miles (3,000 km) across Asia, from Afghanistan to Myanmar, and range from 150 to 210 miles (250 to 350 km) wide. This great mountain range originated via plate tectonics—when the Indian plate collided with Eurasia. The Himalayas are the youngest mountains in the world, which accounts in part for their great height. At present they are still growing as the Indian Plate continues to push into the Asian continent at the rate of about 2.3 inches (6 cm) annually. The Indian subcontinent is believed to have penetrated at least 1,240 miles (2,000 km) into Asia thus far, folding and uplifting the crust of the Earth as it goes.

UNDERSTANDING MONSOONS

Monsoons are seasonal winds that blow from the south from April to October, bringing torrential rains. Then they reverse direction and blow from the north for the remaining six months. During the wet season, moist air is cooled as it blows over rising land, forcing abundant rainfall on the windward side of mountain ranges.

Monsoons are caused primarily by the much greater annual variation in temperature over large areas of land than over large areas of adjacent ocean water. In Asia the air temperature over Siberia increases in the summer, and the resulting hot air rises, causing a huge low-pressure area over the land. Wind carrying moisture from above the Indian Ocean rushes in to fill the low-pressure void. As the air moves from sea-level altitude over the ocean to the higher altitudes over the land, it rises, cools, and releases its moisture in the form of rain. In the winter the reverse happens. Cold air over Siberia creates high pressure. Warmer air over the ocean causes low pressure, and the cold, dry air over the continents blows in from the north.

Afghanistan. The Himalayas begin in Afghanistan as a spur known as the Hindu Kush. Here the mountains reach an elevation 20,000 feet (6,100 m), and many are snow-covered year-round and contain glaciers. The climate is typical of an arid or

GEO GEM

The Caucasus Republics

Armenia, Azerbaijan, and Georgia are three former Soviet states that are now independent nations located southwest of the Caucasus Mountains.

semiarid steppe, with cold winters and hot, dry summers. The mountain regions of the northeast are subarctic with dry and cold winters. The desert is subject to violent sandstorms during the dry winter months. Bordered by China, Russia, Pakistan, and Iran, Afghanistan is completely landlocked.

Pakistan. Pakistan is bordered by Afghanistan, China, and India on the east. It is mostly a hot, dry desert climate, but conditions are temperate in the northwest and arctic in the north. The terrain includes the flat Indus plain in the east, mountains in the north and northwest, and a high-elevation plateau in the west. About one quarter of the land is arable. Pakistan has extensive natural-gas reserves.

Nepal and Bhutan. These two independent countries are mostly mountainous, with tropical jungles in the south where they border on fertile Ganges Plains. The highest peak in the world, **Mount Everest** (elevation 29,035 feet/8,850 m), is in Nepal.

THE OVERPOPULATED INDIAN SUBCONTINENT

The seventh largest nation in the world in terms of area, India is second only to the United States in terms of arable land. But as the second most populous country in the world, it has extreme poverty and a lack of infrastructure to support the burgeoning population. Although India has some very large cities, including the capital, Mumbai, almost 80 percent of the population lives in rural areas. Rapid economic development is increasing the economic disparity within the country. India and surrounding nations are divided geographically into three major regions north to south: the Himalayas, the Ganges Plain in the north, and the peninsula in the south.

The Himalayas

The Himalayas play a significant role in India's climate, blocking the flow of air from the north. As a result, India's monsoon climate is very hot. Also, the Himalayas are the source of India's great rivers: the Ganges and the Indus.

The Ganges Plain

The Ganges Plain, which stretches from the Indus to the Ganges River Delta, is almost completely flat and immensely fertile, fed by snowmelt from the high peaks. Streams and rivers from the mountains have carved up the northern edge of the plains into rough gullies and crevices. The climate is monsoon, with cooler temperatures in the north.

Bangladesh, formerly East Pakistan, lies within the Ganges plain. An extremely poor, densely populated country, Bangladesh is low-lying, fertile, and well watered. But about one third of the land floods annually during the rainy season, hampering economic development and bringing many health problems via disease and toxic pesticides carried on surface water.

The Peninsula

South of the plains is the peninsula, a varied region of low plateaus and river valleys. It includes desert, salt marshes,

ISTANBUL (NOT CONSTANTINOPLE)

Istanbul is the largest city in Turkey and the fifth largest city in the world, with a population of 12.8 million. It played a key role in history when it went by the names of Byzantium and Constantinople and was the capital of the Roman Empire, Byzantine Empire, the Latin Empire, and the Ottoman Empire.

Today Istanbul is the cultural and financial center of Turkey and the only city in the world straddling two continents: Asia and Europe. It is also situated near the North Anatolian Fault, which marks the boundary between the African and Eurasian plates. This fault zone has been responsible for several deadly earthquakes throughout the city's history, including one in 1999 that left 17,000 people dead.

and the great lava expanse called the **Deccan Plateau**. Coastal plains border the plateau. The coastal plains on the eastern side are wider than those in the west and heavily populated. Most of southern India, particularly inland, is hot and dry. Temperatures can reach as high as 120°F (49°C).

Monsoons from June through September produce severe storms with huge quantities of rain, particularly on the western and northeastern coasts. Some areas get over 100 inches (25 cm) of rain each year.

The teardrop-shaped island of **Sri Lanka,** formerly known as Ceylon, lies south of India. A former colony of Great Britain, Sri Lanka is famous for its tea plantations. A long-standing conflict with Tamil Tiger rebels has left the country with large foreign debt. Agriculture, textiles, and tourism are major industries.

Off the southwestern tip of the peninsula are the **Maldives,** a group of about 1,200 islands and atolls, just north of the equator in the Indian Ocean. Only 200 of the islands are inhabited. The **flattest country** on Earth, these islands reach an altitude of only about 8 feet (2.4 m) above sea level at their highest point. The absolute number and identity of the islands varies because old islands are constantly submerged and new ones created. White sandy beaches, deep-blue lagoons, and coral reefs are part of the beauty of this nation.

GEOPOLITICS: GULF OIL RESOURCES AND THE MIDDLE EAST

There is no strict definition of which countries make up the Middle East, which at various times and by various groups has been called the Near East, the Levant, West Asia, and the Gulf Region. Generally it is made up of the countries of the **Arabian Peninsula** and those that border the **Persian Gulf.** This includes **Turkey, Syria, Jordan, Lebanon, Israel, Saudi Arabia, Yemen, Oman, United Arab Emirates (UAE), Qatar, Bahrain, Kuwait, Iraq,** and **Iran.** There is no state of Palestine—only territories (the Gaza Strip and portions of the West Bank) that are controlled by the Palestinian National Authority.

The Middle East famously includes the **"cradle of Western civilization"** in the Tigris-Euphrates river basin, which is now Iraq. Islam is the dominant religion in the region, with its two holiest cities—Mecca and Medina—both in Saudi Arabia. Jerusalem in Israel is also an important religious site for Jews and Christians. The region has been the locus for religious conflict over the centuries.

Many countries located around the Persian Gulf have large quantities of crude oil, which is one reason the area is so politically sensitive today.

Terrain. Most of the land in the region can be described as high rugged mountains and plateaus and dry lowland areas. The desert of the Arabian Peninsula is so inhospitable that it has been given the name the Empty Quarter. Other significant deserts exist throughout the region.

Climate. The Middle East generally has an arid and hot climate, with several major rivers providing irrigation to support agriculture in limited areas. In the desert areas rainfall is low, averaging about 4 inches (10 cm) per year, and temperatures range greatly. Mountainous regions in Iraq, Turkey, and Iran experience freezing temperatures and heavy snows in winter. Along the coasts of the Mediterranean Sea, as well as the Black and Caspian seas, the water moderates the temperature extremes of the desert, resulting in a climate that is similar to that of southern Italy and California.

 **GEO GEM**

The Little Ice Age

Mount Tambora erupted in Indonesia in 1815, causing what became known as the Little Ice Age. Volcanic ash in the atmosphere blocked out incoming solar radiation, and global temperatures plummeted. The year 1816 was known as the Year without a Summer. Frost and snow were reported during June and July of 1816 in New England and Northern Europe.

Natural Resources. The Middle East is rich in **petroleum.** The proven oil reserves of Saudi Arabia alone are known to be 25 percent of the world's total; those of Iraq, Iran, and Kuwait constitute another 25 percent. Overall, it is estimated that more than 62 percent of all proven oil reserves are found in the Middle East and North Africa. Furthermore, Middle Eastern oil is both cheap to produce and of high quality. Saudi Arabia also has gold and silver mines thought to date from ancient times.

Chapter 6

Europe

You might not agree that Europe is a continent. Some geographers call it a peninsula that is part of Eurasia. But the area is culturally distinct from Asia—even if Russia falls within both Europe and Asia. So we will consider Europe a continent, separated from Asia by the Ural and Caucasus mountains.

Europe is small and diverse, a cluster of islands and peninsulas with surprisingly few landlocked nations and plenty of coastlines, rivers, mountains, and arable land. Most of Europe lies within 300 miles (483 km) of a seacoast, so it is no surprise that seafaring has helped shaped the history—and colonizing efforts—of the continent.

From ancient Greece to the Roman Empire to Britannia's rule of the waves, Europe once played a dominating role in world affairs. But those days seem to be over.

A FULLY DEVELOPED CONTINENT

Europe has been fully settled for centuries. Its agriculture and industry are fully developed. Europe was once covered with temperate forests, but little of that remains. The land has been so intensively grazed and farmed for centuries that there is very little land that has not been affected by humans. Few areas of untouched wilderness are left, except in Scandinavia and northern Russia.

In the north the **Gulf Stream** and the **North Atlantic Stream,** currents in the Atlantic, moderate what would otherwise be an arctic climate. Southern Europe has a Mediterranean climate, with frequent summer droughts. Most of the mountains, including the Alps and the Pyrenees, run east to west, allowing wind to carry large masses of moisture-laden water from the ocean into the interior. A semiarid climate is found in small regions of central Spain and near the Caspian Sea. These dry regions receive only enough rain to grow small plants. There are no true deserts in Europe, and Europeans are hoping that it stays that way.

THE LEGACY OF THE ICE AGE: NORTHERN EUROPE

The great seafaring Nordic countries (**Denmark, Finland, Iceland, Norway,** and **Sweden**) have miles and miles and miles of coastline. But don't think hot sun and sandy beaches. Parts of northern Europe lie within the Arctic Circle. Norway and

(continued on page 114)

THE COUNTRIES OF EUROPE

COUNTRY	CAPITAL	AREA*	POPULATION**
Albania	Tirana	11	3.6
Andorra	Andorra la Vella	0.2	0.1
Austria	Vienna	32	8.2
Belarus	Minsk	80	9.6
Belgium	Brussels	12	10.4
Bosnia & Herzegovina	Sarajevo	20	4.6
Bulgaria	Sofia	43	7.2
Croatia	Zagreb	22	4.5
Cyprus	Nicosia	4	0.8
Czech Republic	Prague	30	10.2
Denmark	Copenhagen	17	5.5
Estonia	Tallinn	17	1.3
Finland	Helsinki	131	5.2
France	Paris	213	60.2
Germany	Berlin	138	82.3
Greece	Athens	51	10.7
Hungary	Budapest	36	9.9
Iceland	Reykjavik	40	0.3
Ireland	Dublin	27	4.2

COUNTRY	CAPITAL	AREA*	POPULATION**
Italy	Rome	116	58.1
Latvia	Riga	25	2.2
Liechtenstein	Vaduz	0.1	0.03
Lithuania	Vilnius	25	3.6
Luxembourg	Luxembourg City	1	0.5
Macedonia, the Former Yugoslav Republic of	Skopje	10	2.1
Malta	Valletta	0.1	0.4
Moldova	Chisinau	13	4.3
Monaco	Monaco	0.001	0.03
Montenegro	Podgorica	5	0.7
Netherlands	Amsterdam	16	16.7
Norway	Oslo	125	4.7
Poland	Warsaw	125	38.5
Portugal	Lisbon	36	10.7
Romania	Bucharest	92	22.2
San Marino	San Marino	0.02	0.03
Serbia	Belgrade	34	7.4
Slovakia	Bratislava	19	5.5

THE COUNTRIES OF EUROPE *(continued)*

COUNTRY	CAPITAL	AREA*	POPULATION**
Slovenia	Ljubljana	8	2.0
Spain	Madrid	195	40.5
Sweden	Stockholm	174	9.0
Switzerland	Berne	16	7.6
Turkey	Ankara	299	76.8
Ukraine	Kiev	233	45.7
United Kingdom	London	95	61.1

*in thousands of square miles
**in millions

Sweden make up the Scandinavian Peninsula, the largest peninsula in Europe. The spectacular fjords that make up a lot of the coastline make for great sightseeing but not much sunbathing. Iceland is a volcanic island, and its numerous hot springs provide much spa-type pleasure, but again no beaches.

Although the last Ice Age ended more than 8,000 years ago, its effects can still be seen today where the moving ice (glaciers) carved out the northern landscape. Erratic boulders, U-shaped valleys, drumlins, eskers, kettle lakes, bedrock striations, and fjords are typical features of the region—and the typical results of glacial activity.

Most of Norway and northern Sweden is mountainous, but in southern Sweden, lowlands slope gently to the Baltic Sea and provide fertile lands for agriculture. In both countries and in Finland, Ice Age glaciers left behind thousands of freshwater lakes. The main part of Denmark is the peninsula of Jutland, which extends into the North Sea toward Norway and Sweden. On Jutland's west side, glaciers deposited sand and gravel to create a flat landscape but carved fjords into the slightly higher coastline on the east. Flat plains or low hills make up most of the interior.

The weight of the ice sheets was so great that they actually deformed the Earth's crust and mantle. After the ice sheets melted, the ice-covered land **rebounded,** or lifted back up. In Sweden, Lake Mälaren was once an arm of the Baltic Sea, but as the land rebounded, the lake was cut off from the sea, eventually becoming a freshwater lake in about the twelfth century. Rebounding is still going on today.

Norway is a long, narrow country on the western edge of the Scandinavian Peninsula, with 50,000 islands off the much-indented coastline. Its highest point, Galdhöpiggen, is more than 8,000 feet (2,400 m) above sea level. The mountains in northern Norway are home to the largest glacier on mainland Europe, Jostedal Glacier. A very small percentage of the land is arable as a consequence of **glacial scouring,** which literally scraped away the soil from the land. The glaciers also deepened river valleys, which were invaded by the sea when the ice melted, creating the famous fjords. In the south the glaciers deposited sediment, creating a very chaotic landscape.

The mountains of Norway are part of the same chain of mountains that cover Scotland, Ireland, cross the Atlantic

 **GEO GEM**

The Prime Meridian

The prime meridian (0° longitude) runs through Great Britain, France, and Spain.

Ocean, and form the Appalachian Mountains of North America.

Most of Europe's many lakes are in the north. Finland is the chief lake country—about 9 percent of its area is water.

The climate in the northern reaches of the peninsula is subpolar and tundra, with extremely cold, long winters, similar to the climate of Alaska. There are cool marine climates in northwestern, southern, and southwestern coastal areas and a humid continental climate in the central portion. The region is rich in timber, iron, and copper, with the best farmland found in southern Sweden. Large petroleum and natural-gas deposits have been found off Norway's coast in the North Sea and the Atlantic Ocean.

WESTERN EUROPE

Exactly what constitutes Western Europe is up for debate. It has many definitions, including this one: Western Europe is the part of Europe that did not come under Soviet Russia's influence during the cold war. By this definition Germany and Greece are both

THE HOT SPRINGS OF ICELAND

The island country of Iceland is basically one big volcano, formed over millions of years as molten rock bubbled up from the seafloor. The porous rock underlying the region sponges up hundreds of inches of rain every year and heats it below ground. Using this energy is simply a matter of digging a well, drawing the hot water to the surface, and building a power plant on top. Not only is the heat source free, but the resulting electricity is carbon-neutral. Iceland ranks fourteenth in the world for geothermal resources but is the highest per-capita producer of geothermal power.

parts of Western Europe. By other definitions, Greece belongs with the other nations of the Balkan nations, and Germany belongs in Central Europe. For this discussion let's say Western Europe includes Andorra, Austria, Belgium, France, Ireland, Italy, Luxembourg, Malta, Monaco, the Netherlands, Portugal, San Marino, Spain, United Kingdom, and Vatican City.

United Kingdom and Ireland. The United Kingdom is made up of **England,** **Scotland,** **Wales,** and **Northern Ireland.** The **Republic of Ireland** is a separate nation. Separated from mainland Europe by the North Sea and the English Channel, this region has a temperate climate with ample rain.

 **GEO GEM**

The Former Yugoslavia

Like the U.S.S.R. (Union of Soviet Socialist Republics), Yugoslavia fell victim to the collapse of communism in the late 1980s. It had always been a federation of republics, and these are now the separate countries of Bosnia and Herzegovina, Croatia, Montenegro, Serbia, Slovenia, and the grandly named Former Yugoslav Republic of Macedonia.

Kosovo, once part of Serbia, has declared itself independent, but its status is disputed.

France. South across the English Channel lies France. It is a leading producer of wine, despite the fact that two thirds of the land is covered by mountains and hills. There are seven named mountain ranges, the largest being the Pyrenees along the border with Spain, and the Alps along the Swiss and Italian borders. **Mont Blanc** in the Alps is the **tallest mountain** in Europe (elevation 15,782 feet/ 4,811 m). France also touches three major bodies of water: the Atlantic Ocean, Mediterranean Sea, and the English Channel. Long before Disney

> ### 🌍 GEO GEM
>
> #### The Lowlands
> Although often called Holland, the Netherlands is the official name of the country located between Germany and Belgium. The word translates as "the lowlands" in Dutch. One third of the Netherlands is below sea level. The Netherlands' highest point is about 1,000 feet (304 m) above sea level.

World, the Mediterranean coast, also known as the Côte d'Azur or French Riviera, was the modern world's number one tourist destination.

Iberian Peninsula. The Pyrennes Mountains form the northern boundary of the peninsula, which includes **Spain, Portugal,** and the tiny mountain country of **Andorra.** The north is the wettest region, the central region is dry, and the coasts are popular resort areas. Spain is a leading producer of olive oil, and Portugal is the world's leading producer of cork. At the southern tip of Spain is the British territory of **Gibraltar,** which lies a mere 8 miles (13 km) from Africa. Desertification is a growing problem in the region.

The Low Countries. Belgium, the Netherlands, and **Luxembourg** make up the low countries, so named because much of the land is at or below sea level. They are also called the Benelux countries (a combination of the names). The land in this area is mostly flat, with the soil mainly composed of either glacier-deposited sand, gravel, and clay or of silt laid down by rivers after the last Ice Age. Since the Middle Ages, the Dutch have built dikes—large banks of earth and stone—to hold back water and reclaim land from the sea. These reclaimed lands, called **polders,** once were drained and kept dry by the use of windmills. Today other power sources continually run pumps to remove seawater. Polders provide hundreds of thousands of acres for farming and settlement.

The Italian Peninsula. The boot-shaped Italian peninsula is surrounded by the Ligurian, Tyrrhenian, Mediterranean, Ionian, and Adriatic seas. Off the western tip of the boot is the island of **Sicily;** the islands of **Sardinia** and **Corsica** (part of France) are farther north, in the Tyrrhenian Sea. Between Sicily and Africa is the tiny independent nation of **Malta.** Two other independent states are found within the borders of Italy: **San Marino** and **Vatican City.** At the top of the peninsula is the Alps, forming a border that separates Italy from France, Switzerland, Austria, and Slovenia. The Apennine Mountains run down the center of the peninsula like a spine. Italy has Europe's only active volcanoes, **Mount Etna** (in Sicily) and **Vesuvius.** Italy's main export is cars, and tourism is a growing industry.

THE MAGNIFICENT ALPS

The Bavarian Alps dominate the southern part of **Germany,** bordering the Alpine countries of **Austria, Liechtenstein,** and **Switzerland.** Germany is the most populous nation in Europe. Although highly industrialized, Germany has a temperate climate and fertile soil; about 34 percent of its land is arable.

The Alps divide northern and southern Europe, but they have allowed both peaceful trade and enemy invasions over the centuries. The **Danube,** the **longest river** in Europe has its headwaters in southwest Germany and flows southeast through **Austria, Hungary, Serbia,** and **Romania** to the Black Sea. It has been a major trade route since the Middle Ages. Other rivers with their headwaters in the Alps include the **Rhône** and the **Po.**

The Alps were formed by tectonic plate action, in this case

by the African plate colliding with the Eurasian plate, causing the land to fold and uplift, a process that continues today. Glaciers that covered the land during the ice ages further sculpted the region. Were it not for the glaciers, the Alps would be closer in height to the Himalayas.

The Alps extend in a crescent about 750 miles (1,200 km) from the Mediterranean coast between France and Italy to Vienna and cover more than 80,000 square miles (207,000 sq km). Several peaks rise above 10,000 feet (3,000 m). Glaciers form a permanent snow and ice covering of about 1,500 square miles (3,900 sq km), mostly at elevations above 10,000 feet (3,000 m).

EASTERN EUROPE

Eastern Europe is a region of great ethnic, economic, and political diversity. The region includes former Soviet states and former Warsaw Pact nations. (The Warsaw Pact was established in 1955 to counter the threat from the NATO countries and was dissolved at the end of the cold war in 1991.) Eastern Europe stretches from the Baltic Sea in the northwest (Lithuania, Latvia, and Estonia) to the Black Sea in the southeast and includes Poland, Hungary, Ukraine, Belarus, and Slovakia.

The Baltic States. The Baltic Way was a peaceful independence movement in **Lithuania, Latvia,** and **Estonia** between 1987 and 1991. In 1989, during the "Singing Revolution," in a landmark demonstration

---

🌎 GEO GEM

Smallest Country

Monaco is the smallest country, in terms of area, in the United Nations. It exists on a grand total of 1 square mile (1.6 sq km) of French Riviera coastline. It is also the most densely populated; it packs 33,000 people into that tiny area.

for more independence, a human chain of more than 2 million people was formed, stretching through all three countries. These nations all had similar experiences of foreign occupation and similar aspirations for regaining independence. The Estonian Sovereignty Declaration was issued on November 16, 1988; Lithuania became independent in 1990; Latvia became independent from the Soviet Union in 1991.

Former Soviet States. Belarus has a strong central government and remains economically tied to Russia. About 70 percent of the nuclear fallout from the 1986 accident at the Chernobyl nuclear power plant in nearby Ukraine landed in Belarus; about 20 percent of its land remains contaminated. **Ukraine** is the largest European nation (when Russia is not counted) and has abundant farmland with fertile black soil and plenty of water. It was once the "breadbasket" of the Soviet Union and is also rich in mineral resources.

Warsaw Pact Nations. Slovakia separated from the **Czech Republic** in 1993 in what was called a "velvet divorce," following on the heels of Czechoslovakia's "velvet revolution," in which it gained its independence from the Soviet Union in 1989. **Hungary** and **Poland** are also nations moving to more progressive market economies. Poland's central location and mostly flat terrain historically has made it the battleground for countless European wars.

Location Is Everything: The Balkan States

Because its location in southeastern Europe separates Western Europe from the Middle East, the mountainous Balkan region has been the site of many wars. Following the wars, borders have not always been drawn with sensitivity to ethnic divisions,

> **🌎 GEO GEM**
>
> **Fjord**
> A fjord is a steep-sided inlet cut into mountains by glaciers, creating spectacular scenery. Norway is famous for its fjords, but fjords also occur in Chile and New Zealand.

so there have been more wars. In modern times there were major redefinition of borders following the breakup of the Ottoman Empire, World War I, and the breakup of the Soviet Union.

The exact definition of the Balkans is loose; it was originally used to describe the area that remained under Turkish rule after the fall of the Ottoman Empire. Since the Balkan States were formed, the word "balkanize" has come to mean "to divide a region into small, hostile states." Today the Balkan States is considered: **Albania, Bosnia** and **Herzegovina, Bulgaria, Croatia, Greece, Kosovo, Macedonia, Moldava, Montenegro, Romania, Serbia,** and **Slovenia.**

The Balkan peninsula is surrounded by the Black Sea, the Sea of Marmara, and several arms of the Mediterranean, including the Aegean, Ionian, and Adriatic seas. It is a mountainous region, and the mountains have generally acted to isolate ethnic groups and impede national unity.

STRADDLING CONTINENTS

Europe or Asia? When it comes to the continents where **Russia** and **Turkey** lie, you get to choose.

Russia is so big it stretches across 11 time zones. Its two largest cities—Moscow, the capital, and St. Petersburg—are both located on the western (European) end. A little more than three quarters of Russia's entire population lives in European Russia, which is no surprise, considering the reputation Siberia has in the eastern part of the country. The Ural Mountains run north to south through

THE FORMER SOVIET UNION

The country we used to call the Union of Soviet Socialist Republics (actually, we called it the U.S.S.R., or Soviet Russia) came into being in 1922 after the Russian Revolution and the civil war that followed. At the time, it was the largest country in the world—a massive 8.6 million square miles (22.3 million km).

Soviet Russia started to collapse in the late 1980s and formally ceased to exist in 1991. The new nations that have emerged as a result are split between Europe and Asia. The countries in Europe included Belarus, Estonia, Latvia, Lithuania, Moldova, and Ukraine. The countries in Asia include Armenia, Azerbaijan, Georgia, Kazakhstan, Kyrgyzstan, Russia, Tajikistan, Turkmenistan, and Uzbekistan. And even having lost all this real estate, the Russian Federation remains the largest country in the world in terms of area.

western Russia, from the coast of the Arctic Ocean to the Ural River and northwestern Kazakhstan, and the eastern side is usually considered the natural boundary between Europe and Asia. So you might be leaning toward calling Russia a European nation. But 77 percent of its land is in Asia, and therein lies the dilemma.

Likewise, about 97 percent of Turkey is located in a region known as Anatolia, a high central plateau with narrow coastal plains that is located in Asia. The other 3 percent, eastern Turkey in the Balkan peninsula, is separated from Asian Turkey by the Bosphorus, the Sea of Marmara, and the Dardanelles (which together form a water link between the Black Sea and the Mediterranean). Turkey is mountainous and the source of several important rivers, including the Euphrates, Tigris, and Aras. Mount Ararat, a dormant volcano, is the highest peak in Turkey at 16,946 feet (5,165 m). The region has frequent earthquakes, and fault lines run through Turkey. So is Turkey in Europe or Asia? You decide.

Chapter 7

Africa

*The second largest continent (11.7 million square miles/19 million sq km), Africa accounts for about 20 percent of the Earth's landmass. It is the most tropical of all the continents. Surrounded by water on all sides, it was once connected to Asia in its northeast corner by the Sinai Peninsula, where the Suez Canal now connects the Red Sea and the Mediterranean. Both the **equator** and the **prime meridian** run through the continent, and more of the continent's landmass is in its northern half. There are relatively few islands off Africa's coast; **Madagascar** is by far the largest.*

Africa's population of 922 million is the second largest in the world. Its people are divided into several thousand different ethnic groups speaking an estimated 2,000 different languages.

It's a Jungle Out There

It's true. Africa is home to the **second largest rainforest** in the world, most of it along the equator and in the basin of the Congo River. Is it rainforest or jungle? Well, there is a

technical difference, but the terms are used loosely, as though jungles exist in Africa but rainforests are found in South America, or jungles are old-school and rainforests are the politically correct term. Africa has both rainforest and jungle. And it has so much more.

The continent of Africa was called "the dark continent" by Europeans who made haste to colonize the New World as soon as it was "discovered" in the fifteenth and sixteenth centuries. But Africa, which was closer geographically, wasn't exploited until the 1800s.

Why was that? Geography.

First there was the problem of an unusually smooth coastline with few natural harbors. Once landed in new territory, old-school explorers generally found travel by water the easiest route to take into the interior. Not so in Africa, where the rivers are not easily navigated due to a mix of rapids and waterfalls. Also, sand deposits in slow-moving areas downstream from the rapids tended to beach any boat that was not flat-bottomed.

The overland routes were equally difficult since most of the continent consists of vast plateaus of varying elevations. The plateaus' edges, especially the eastern and the southern ones, are marked by sharp escarpments (mountainous walls) that descend to narrow plains along the coast.

(continued on page 132)

THE COUNTRIES OF AFRICA

COUNTRY	CAPITAL	AREA*	POPULATION**
Algeria	Algiers	920	34.2
Angola	Luanda	481	12.8
Benin	Porto Novo	43	8.8
Botswana	Gaborone	225	2.0
Burkina Faso	Ouagadougou	106	15.7
Burundi	Bujumbura	9.0	
Cameroon	Yaoundé	184	18.9
Cape Verde	Praia	2	0.4
Central African Republic	Bangui	241	4.5
Chad	N'Djamena	496	10.3
Comoros	Moroni	0.9	0.8
Congo, Democratic Republic of the (DRC)	Kinshasa	905	68.7
Congo, Republic of the	Brazzaville	132	4.0
Côte d'Ivoire	Yamoussoukro	125	20.6
Djibouti	Djibouti City	0.5	
Egypt	Cairo	387	83.1
Equatorial Guinea	Malabo	11	0.6

COUNTRY	CAPITAL	AREA*	POPULATION**
Eritrea	Asmara	45	5.6
Ethiopia	Addis Ababa	426	85.2
Gabon	Libreville	103	1.5
Gambia	Banjul	4	1.8
Ghana	Accra	92	23.9
Guinea	Conakry	95	10.1
Guinea-Bissau	Bissau	14	1.5
Kenya	Nairobi	224	39.0
Lesotho	Maseru	12	2.1
Liberia	Monrovia	43	3.4
Libya	Tripoli	679	6.3
Madagascar	Antananarivo	227	20.7
Malawi	Lilongwe	46	14.3
Mali	Bamako	479	12.7
Mauritania	Nouakchott	396	3.1
Mauritius	Port Louis	0.8	1.3
Morocco	Rabat	172	34.9
Mozambique	Maputo	309	21.7
Namibia	Windhoek	318	2.1
Niger	Niamey	489	15.3

THE COUNTRIES OF AFRICA *(continued)*

COUNTRY	CAPITAL	AREA*	POPULATION**
Nigeria	Abuja	357	149.2
Rwanda	Kigali	10	10.5
São Tomé & Príncipe	São Tomé	0.4	0.2
Senegal	Dakar	76	13.7
Seychelles	Victoria	0.2	0.1
Sierra Leone	Freetown	28	6.4
Somalia	Mogadishu	246	9.8
South Africa	Pretoria	471	49.0
South Sudan, Republic of	Juba	385	9.0
Sudan	Khartoum	5822	32.0
Swaziland	Mbabane	7	1.1
Tanzania, United Republic of	Dodoma	365	41.0
Togo	Lomé	22	6.0
Tunisia	Tunis	63	10.5
Uganda	Kampala	93	32.4
Zambia	Lusaka	291	11.9
Zimbabwe	Harare	151	11.4

*in thousands of square miles
**in millions

THAT WAS THEN, THIS IS NOW

Do you have trouble remembering the names of Africa's nations? Maybe it is because so many have changed since you first learned them. There was a lot of name changing when former European colonies gained independence, and then more name changing from internal upheavals.

Benin: formerly Dahomey
Botswana: formerly Bechuanaland
Burkina Faso: formerly Upper Volta
Burundi: formerly joined with Rwanda to form Ruanda-Urundi
Congo, Democratic Republic of the: formerly Zaire, before that the Belgian Congo
Congo, Republic of the: formerly the French Congo
Côte d'Ivoire: formerly the Ivory Coast
Djibouti: formerly the French Territory of the Afars and the Issas
Eritrea: gained independence from Ethiopia in 1993
Ethiopia: formerly Abyssinia Empire or Ethiopian Empire
Guinea: formerly French Guinea
Guinea-Bissau: formerly Portuguese Guinea
Lesotho: formerly Basutoland
Malawi: formerly Nyasaland
Mali: formerly French Sudan
Namibia: formerly South West Africa
Rwanda: formerly joined with Burundi to form Ruanda-Urundi
Tanzania, United Republic of: formed in 1964 from a union of Tanganyika and Zanzibar
Zambia: formerly Northern Rhodesia
Zimbabwe: formerly Southern Rhodesia, then from 1964–79 Rhodesia

Then there are the deserts. Africa has some of the hottest, harshest deserts on earth: the **Sahara** in the north, **Namib** and **Kalahari** in the south. In the center of the continent is the **Great Rift Valley**, a geological fault system that includes perpendicular cliffs and mountain ridges.

Back to the Jungle

About 20 percent of Africa is covered by rainforest (and jungle), mostly located in central and western Africa. However, there are patches of rainforest in eastern and southern parts as well—in **Ethiopia, Kenya, Tanzania, Mozambique,** and **Zimbabwe.**

The Congo River Basin is the second largest rainforest in the world at 1.4 million square miles (3.6 million sq km). It dominates the landscape of the **Democratic Republic of the Congo** and much of neighboring **Republic of the Congo,** and it stretches into **Cameroon, the Central African Republic, Zambia, Equatorial Guinea,** and **Gabon.** Running through the rainforest is the Congo River, the second longest river in Africa. The Congo Basin contains an estimated 70 percent of the vegetation on the entire continent and is the most biologically diverse area, with more than 600 tree species and 10,000 animal species, among them gorillas, chimpanzees, and elephants.

Unfortunately, since the 1980s, Africa has experienced the greatest rate of rainforest destruction of any region on the planet, and the Congo has one of the world's most

🌎 GEO GEM

The Gift of the Nile

Egypt, which has been called "the gift of the Nile," is essentially a narrow ribbon of densely settled valley carved out of the desert. It is estimated that over 95 percent of Egypt's population is concentrated on 5 percent of its territory.

threatened ecosystems. Commercial logging, slash-and-burn clearing for subsistence agriculture, and widespread political unrest have all combined to devastate the forests and displace the native forest dwellers.

SAND DUNES AND DRY LANDS

The second largest desert in the world, the **Sahara,** pretty much covers the northern end of the Africa from the Atlantic Ocean in the west to the Red Sea in the east, a distance of some 3,000 miles (4,828 km). From north to south, it starts at the Mediterranean Sea on the north and extends 1,200 miles (1,931 km) to the south, almost into central Africa. It is part of the landscape of **Morocco, Algeria, Tunisia, Libya, Egypt, Mauritania, Mali, Niger, Chad, Ethiopa, Eritrea,** and **Somalia.**

There's no place on Earth as consistently hot as the Sahara, which has an average annual temperature of 86°F (30°C). During the hottest months, temperatures can exceed 122°F (50°C), with the highest temperature ever recorded in Aziziyah, Libya—136°F (58°C).

The central part of the desert, known as the Libyan Sahara Desert, is considered the most arid part. Rain is almost totally absent, and few oases exist. The land looks like a classic desert landscape with sand dunes up to 400 feet (122 m) or more in height. The Sahara has plenty of other wind- and sand-sculpted features: sand seas called ergs, barren stone plateaus, gravel plains, dry valleys, salt flats, and rocky highlands.

🌐 **GEO GEM**

Southern Sudan's New Name

After its recent secession from the Sudan, Southern Sudan is now officially named the Republic of South Sudan. Other candidates were Azania, Nile Republic, and Kush Republic, but its new name was chosen out of familiarity and convenience.

There are also several mountain ranges within the Sahara, including volcanoes. The highest peak is **Emi Koussi,** a shield volcano that rises to 11,204 feet (3,415 m) in northern Chad. The lowest point in the Sahara is in Egypt's **Qattera Depression,** at 436 feet (133 m) below sea level. Water is always the issue in a desert. Most of the water found in the Sahara today is in the form of seasonal or intermittent streams. The only permanent river in the desert is the Nile River, which flows from central Africa to the Mediterranean Sea. Other water in the Sahara is found in underground aquifers. In areas where this water reaches the surface, there are oases. Where there are oases, there are towns and people.

The Kalahari and Namibia Deserts

The Kalahari Desert and the Namibia Desert are found in the southern part of the continent. The Kalahari varies from semiarid conditions with up to 20 inches (500 mm) of rain annually to arid conditions, where there is virtually no rain at all—mostly in the southeast. The Kalahari includes parts of **Botswana, South Africa,** and **Namibia.**

The Namib Desert, an arid coastal region in **Namibia** in southwestern Africa, extends about 1,000 miles (1,600 km) from **Angola** in the north to **South Africa** in the south. It lies between a high inland plateau and the Atlantic Ocean. Although this desert is primarily rocky, there are vast sand dunes in the central portion. The weather is generally cool because of westerly winds blowing in from the ocean. Diamonds are mined in the alluvial sands along the coast, and mining towns, mostly, account for the small population.

THE ENCROACHING DESERT

South of the Sahara is a narrow belt of semiarid land known as the **Sahel,** a transitional zone between the desert to the north and the savannas to the south. Running between the Atlantic Ocean and the Red Sea, the Sahel covers parts of **Senegal, Mauritania, Mali, Burkina Faso, Algeria, Niger, Nigeria, Chad, Sudan, Somalia, Ethiopia,** and **Eritrea.** The flat, scrubby plains are mostly used for grazing animals. What little rainfall it experiences usually falls in the rainy season—June to September. Agriculture is difficult in the Sahel; however, crops of millet, sorghum, and peanuts are common.

The Sahel is one of the poorest and most environmentally damaged regions on Earth, known for drought, famine, and political crisis. Rainfall has been low, variable, and in decline since the 1970s, when a devastating drought brought on widespread famine. The Sahara

🌐 GEO GEM

Africa's Agriculture

About two thirds of Africa's population is involved in agriculture, although only 6 percent of the land is suitable for crop farming and another 25 percent can be used for grazing.

The majority of the crops are raised in Ethiopia, the Democratic Republic of the Congo, Nigeria, South Africa, and Egypt and include peanuts, coffee, cacao, tea, sugarcane, olives, corn, wheat, rice, millet, sorghum, cassava, plantains, sweet potatoes, potatoes, onions, barley, and dry beans.

is expanding into the Sahel at a rate of about 30 miles (48 km) a year. The chief causes of this desertification are slash-and-burn farming, drought, and overgrazing.

THE NILE: THE WORLD'S LONGEST RIVER

The Nile measures 4,187 miles (6,738 km) from its origin at the Ripon Falls in Burundi to its mouth in the Mediterranean Sea. Along its meandering south-to-north route, it flows through **Uganda, South Sudan, Sudan, Egypt, Ethiopia, Burundi, Kenya, Democratic Republic of the Congo, Tanzania,** and **Rwanda.** The river has two main tributaries: the **White Nile,** which originates at Lake Victoria, and the **Blue Nile,** which originates at Lake Tana in Ethiopia. These rivers meet in Sudan.

The Nile River captures the imagination. It is the foundation of one of the oldest and richest civilizations in the world. Europeans spent years trying to find the source of this mysterious river that snakes its way through the harshest desert in the world. Besides providing water, the Nile famously restores the soil of Egypt's agricultural lands on an annual basis. Every year, the snow in the mountains of East Africa melts, sending a torrent of water that overflows the riverbanks and deposits a black silt that makes excellent topsoil. The ancient Egyptians cultivated and traded wheat, flax, and other crops along the

---

🌐 GEO GEM

Africa's Famous Four-Legged Residents

Africa is famed for its spectacular and unique wildlife. Elephants, rhinoceroses, hippopotamuses, lions, leopards, wildebeests, zebras, countless antelope, gazelles, giraffes, baboons, mountain gorillas, chimpanzees, lemurs, and hyenas are some of Africa's most famous four-legged residents.

Nile. This trading system secured Egypt's diplomatic relationships with other countries and contributed to its economic stability. The Nile also provided a convenient and efficient way to transport people and goods.

According to the World Bank, the Nile River Basin is home to an estimated 160 million people, while almost 300 million live in the 10 countries that share the Nile's waters. Within the next 25 years population within the basin is expected to double, creating an increased demand for water. The allocation of the water has become somewhat contentious since it is based on agreements signed during the colonial era—the 1929 Nile Water Agreement and the 1959 Agreement for the Full Utilization of the Nile. These agreements gave Egypt and Sudan extensive rights over the river's use, ignoring any claims by the upstream countries. However, the upstream countries are facing water scarcity issues, just as Egypt and the Sudan does. Since the 1990s the Nile Basin Initiative has sought to forge an agreement among the countries through which the river flows, but little progress has been made.

THE AFRICAN SAVANNAH

The African **savannah,** rolling grasslands dotted with trees, takes up almost half of the continent, about 5 million square miles. This tropical grassland has wet and dry seasons. It covers parts of **Guinea, Sierra Leone, Liberia, Côte d'Ivoire, Ghana, Togo, Benin, Nigeria, Cameroon, Central African Republic, Chad, South Sudan, Ethiopia, Somalia, the Democratic Republic of the Congo, Angola, Uganda, Rwanda, Burundi, Kenya, Tanzania, Malawi, Zambia, Zimbabwe, Mozambique, Botswana,** and **South Africa.**

The most famous part of the savannah is the **Serengeti Plains** in Tanzania. Here lions, zebras, elephants, giraffes, and many types of ungulates (animals with hooves) graze

THE NILE CROCODILE

One can hardly leave the subject of the Nile River without a nod to the fierce man-eating Nile crocodile. It is estimated that about 200 people become crocodile dinner each year—not just in the Nile Basin but also throughout sub-Saharan Africa and Madagascar; crocodiles also like freshwater marshes and mangrove swamps.

Africa's largest crocodilian can reach a maximum size of about 20 feet (6 m) and can weigh up to 1,650 pounds (730 kg). Their diet is mainly fish, but almost anything looks tasty to a croc— zebras, small hippos, birds, other crocodiles, and humans.

While most reptiles lay their eggs and move on, devoted mom and dad crocs ferociously guard their nests of up to 60 eggs until the eggs hatch, some three months later. Crocs have been seen rolling the eggs gently in their mouths to help hatching babies emerge. The babies are taken to the water by their mother and remain with her for at least two years before reaching maturity.

and hunt. The large grass-eating mammals can survive here because they can move around and eat the plentiful grasses. In turn the carnivores (meat-eaters) find the grass-eaters quite tasty. There are 45 species of mammals, almost 500 species of birds, and 55 species of acacia (trees) in the Serengeti.

THE GREAT RIFT VALLEY

Africa is coming apart at the seams, and the seam is the Great Rift Valley. When the African and Arabian plates separated about 35 million years ago, a huge rift was created in Africa. In a few million years the eastern part of Africa— the eastern portion beyond the valley—will probably split off from the African plate, forming a new plate (the Somali Plate). The sea will invade the gap created by the separation and form a new ocean basin. That's how the Red Sea was formed. It is a widening ocean basin located where the Arabian Peninsula moved away from Africa long ago. The 4,000-mile (6,400-km)-long Great Rift Valley crosses continental lines. It begins in the Beqaa Valley in Lebanon, runs through Israel to the Red Sea, and continues south in Africa to Mozambique. The terrain of the valley ranges from salt flats more than 500 feet (152 meters) below sea level to towering snowcapped mountains. It varies in width from 20 to 60 miles (30 to 100 km).

It should come as no surprise that the Rift Valley is home to 30 active and semi-active volcanoes and countless hot springs along its length. All this geothermal activity is driving the spread of the rift, and the Earth's crust in this region has thinned from the typical 60-mile (100-km) thickness to a mere 12 miles (20 km). Volcanic eruptions are responsible for many of the physical features along the length of the rift—the Ethiopian Highlands, perpendicular cliffs, mountain ridges, rugged valleys, and a series of about 30 very deep lakes along its entire length, including **Lake Tanganyika,** the second deepest lake in the world. Many of Africa's highest mountains border the Rift Valley, including **Mount Kilimanjaro,** the highest at an elevation of 19,340 feet (5895 m).

In eastern Africa the valley divides into the eastern rift and the western rift.

The lakes in the Eastern Rift have no outlet to the sea; these lakes tend to be shallow, with a high mineral content. The shores of these are white from crystallized salt and famous for the large flocks of flamingo that

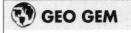

GEO GEM

Home of the Dodo
The island of Mauritius is renowned for having been the only known home of the flightless—and extinct—dodo bird.

feed there. The eastern and western rifts join up again at Lake Nyasa and continue south to Mozambique.

ALL THAT GLITTERS: NATURAL RESOURCES OF AFRICA

Africa is both blessed and cursed with an abundance of natural resources. Resources could play a key role in the development of stable governments and economies, but natural resources have also made Africa the focus of land grabs by other nations and corporations. The politics surrounding control of natural resources has a long history of disrupting communities and increasing armed conflict.

Oil. Sub-Saharan Africa is home to eight oil exporters: Nigeria, Angola, Republic of the Congo, Gabon, Equatorial Guinea, Cameroon, Chad, the Democratic Republic of Congo, and Sudan. Nigeria is the largest producer in Africa, followed by Angola and Sudan. Sub-Saharan Africa has about 7 percent of proven world oil reserves, mostly off west and central Africa's Atlantic coast. The United States is the largest importer of African oil, with China second. About 50 percent of foreign investment in Africa is related to petroleum resources.

Natural Gas. Africa has rich and underdeveloped natural-gas resources. It has the fastest growth rate in natural-gas production worldwide. Natural gas is currently being produced in Algeria, Nigeria, Libya, and Egypt.

🌍 GEO GEM

The Horn of Africa

Not a musical instrument, the Horn of Africa is the easternmost projection of the African continent and includes the countries of Eritrea, Djibouti, Ethiopia, and Somalia. The land is plagued with drought and environmental destruction from overgrazing.

MADAGASCAR'S MYSTERY

Madagascar Island, off the eastern coast near Mozambique, is separated from Africa by hundreds of miles of Indian Ocean and 165 million years of evolution—long enough for the plants and animals to evolve into species unlike their African counterparts.

There are 70 varieties of lemur, including one that sounds like a police siren; 150 species of chameleons—the world's largest and smallest; and more than 60 carnivorous pitcher plants. The people of Madagascar arrived about 2,000 years ago via the Indian Ocean; they grow rice in terraced paddies and speak a language with roots similar to those spoken in Southeast Asia.

Minerals. West Africa is one of the fastest-growing gold-producing regions in the world, though South Africa still ranks number one in production. Ghana, Mali, Sierra Leone, Tanzania, Rwanda, and the Democratic Republic of the Congo are also significant sources. The Democratic Republic of the Congo is also rich in copper, cobalt, and coltan, an ore used extensively in cell phones and other electronic devices. Africa has a large share of uranium, bauxite, copper, phosphates, iron ore, chromium, manganese, cobalt, titanium, and platinum.

Diamonds. Diamonds are used for both industry and jewelry, and trade in diamonds is worth more than $37 billion a year. Botswana, the Democratic Republic of the Congo, Sierra Leone, and South Africa hold the biggest reserves.

Timber. Exports to southern European countries still dominate, but China is the principal destination for timber from east Africa, most notably from Mozambique. The exploitation of timber resources in Liberia was a key source of funding in its civil war (1989–1996; 1997–2003). Timber is also important in Côte d'Ivoire, South Africa, and Gabon.

Chapter 8

Australia/Oceania

You probably learned that Australia is a country, an island, and a continent. Most geographers consider it to be part of a larger continent that includes New Zealand and thousands of Pacific islands and coral atolls. Some say the most accurate name is Australia/Oceania; others call it Australasia.

If the "continent" includes the continental shelf, then Tasmania, New Guinea, and nearby islands are part of the continent, since they are part of the same landmass. Those islands are separated by seas that cover the continental shelf—the Arafura Sea and Torres Strait between Australia and New Guinea, and Bass Strait between mainland Australia and Tasmania. But that definition doesn't include New Zealand, which sits on a different landmass.

However you want to define it, Australia or Australia/ Oceania is the smallest continent in terms of size and the second smallest in population. But although the size of Australia/Oceania is small in terms of square miles of dry land, it is spread over 3.3 million square miles (8.5 million sq km) of ocean. Australia/Oceania is located southeast of Asia, surrounded by the Indian and the Pacific oceans.

Don't Get Lost in Oceania!

There's a way of making sense of all this real estate. First, there are the two big nations: New Zealand and Australia. We will look at them separately. Then there are all those islands, but they fall into three easily managed categories. The ending *"esia"* comes from the Greek word for "island," and the three principal **island groups** are Micronesia ("small islands"), Melanesia ("black islands"), and Polynesia ("many islands").

Micronesia. The Federated States of Micronesia consist of four states—Chuuk, Kosrae, Pohnpei, and Yap—which together make up about 700 islands. However, Micronesia is also used more loosely to refer to thousands of equatorial islands in the western Pacific, to the east of the Philippines and north of Melanesia. The group includes Kiribati, the Mariana Islands (home of the Mariana Trench, see page 34), the Caroline Islands, and Nauru. Micronesia islands are all part of the same volcanic zone.

Melanesia. South of Micronesia, north and east of New Guinea, lies Melanesia. Some of its better-known islands are Fiji, New Caledonia, Norfolk Island, the Solomon Islands, and Vanuatu. The name supposedly relates to the dark skins of the original settlers of these islands.

Polynesia. Usually defined as a triangle whose three corners are Hawaii, New Zealand, and Easter Island. Samoa, Tonga, Tuvalu, French Polynesia, and the Cook Islands all fall within

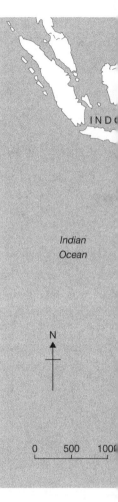

INDO

Indian
Ocean

N

0   500   1000

it. French Polynesia includes the Society Islands, of which the largest and best known is Tahiti.

MAKING SENSE
WITH PLATE TECTONICS—AGAIN

In terms of its physical geography, you can divide up the islands of Oceania based on the geologic processes that formed them.

Australia. Australia sits in the center of the Indo-Australian Plate. Due to its location—away from faults, volcanic action, and plate collisions—it is mostly flat. Erosion accounts for most of its really cool landscape features.

New Zealand and the South Pacific. At the collision boundaries between the Indo-Australian and Pacific plates, New Zealand, Papua New Guinea, and the Solomon Islands were formed. This region is part of the **Pacific Ring of Fire.** The plate collisions are responsible for the formation of mountains like those in New Zealand, which rise more than 10,000 feet (3,000 m).

Volcanic Islands. These islands typically rise from the seafloor through hotspots in the Pacific Ocean basin. Most of these are very small islands with tall mountain ranges, like Fiji and the Solomon Islands.

Coral Reef Islands and Atolls. Coral reef islands, such as Tuvalu, are the last type of landscape found in Oceania. Atolls are islands consisting of a circular coral reef surrounding a lagoon.

TERRITORIES OF AUSTRALIA/OCEANIA

American Samoa: territory of the United States
Cook Islands: self-governing territory of New Zealand
French Polynesia: territory of France
Guam: territory of the United States
Niue: self-governing territory of New Zealand
Northern Mariana Island: commonwealth in political union with the United States
Tokelau: territory of New Zealand
Wallis & Futuna: territory of France

COUNTRIES OF AUSTRALIA/OCEANIA

COUNTRY	CAPITAL	AREA*	POPULATION**
Australia	Canberra	2,989	21.2
Fiji	Suva	7	0.9
Kiribati	Tarawa	0.3	0.1
Marshall Islands	Delap-Uliga-Darrit	0.1	0.1
Micronesia, Federated States of	Palikir	0.3	0.1
Nauru	Yaren	0.01	0.01
New Zealand	Wellington	104	4.2
Palau	Koror	0.2	0.02
Papua New Guinea	Port Moresby	179	6.1
Samoa	Apia	1	0.2
Solomon Islands	Honiara	11	0.6
Tonga	Nuku'alofa	0.3	0.1
Tuvalu	Funafuti	0.01	0.01
Vanuatu	Port Vila	5	0.2

*in thousands of square miles
**in millions

The Island Paradises of the Pacific

Most of the islands of Oceania are in the tropics. They are hot and wet year-round and experience continuous trade winds and occasional hurricanes (called tropical cyclones in Oceania). Tropical rainforests are common. Some of the islands are rich in natural resources, but the majority are not. Many of the island nations do not have enough clean drinking water or food to supply to their citizens. Agriculture in the region includes subsistence agriculture and plantation crops. Fishing is important to Oceania's economies, as is tourism.

The fantasy of giving up the cold, gray, industrialized life of the Western world and finding an island paradise runs deep through Western art and literature. If that's your plan, here are some of the favorite island destinations in Oceania.

Cook Islands. The Cook Islands lie northeast of New Zealand, between French Polynesia and American Samoa. There are 15 major islands divided into two distinct groups: the Southern Cook Islands, and the Northern Cook Islands of coral atolls. The islands were formed by volcanic activity; the northern group is older and consists of six atolls (sunken volcanoes topped by coral growth). The climate is moderate to tropical.

NAME GAME

Do the old names ring a bell?

Kiribati: formerly Gilbert Islands
Nauru: formerly Pleasant Island
Palau: formerly Belau
Samoa, Independent State of: German Samoa and Western Samoa
Tuvalu: formerly Ellice Islands
Vanuatu: formerly New Hebrides

DEATH OF AN ISLAND

Nauru is one of the three great phosphate rock islands in the Pacific Ocean (the others are Banaba in Kiribati and Makatea in French Polynesia). It has very limited natural fresh water resources and no other resources besides phosphate, which is a key ingredient in commercial fertilizer. Intensive phosphate mining during the past 90 years, mainly by a consortium of British, Australian, and New Zealand interests, has left 90 percent of Nauru a literal wasteland.

In anticipation of the exhaustion of Nauru's phosphate deposits, the government wisely invested substantial amounts of phosphate income in trust funds to help provide for Nauru's economic future. But, unwisely, the government spent the trust funds and now faces bankruptcy. Since the government must import all of its food and other necessities, the country with a population of about 9,000 people is completely dependent on foreign aid.

Fiji. An island group about two thirds of the way from Hawaii to New Zealand. Some 400,000 to 500,000 vacation here annually. The waters around Fiji are rich in marine life.

Palau. A group of islands in the North Pacific Ocean, southeast of the Philippines. They vary from the high, mountainous main island of Babelthuap to low coral islands fringed by large barrier reefs.

Papua New Guinea. A group of islands including the eastern half of the island of New Guinea between the Coral Sea and the South Pacific Ocean, east of Indonesia. The islands are mostly mountainous with coastal lowlands and rolling foothills.

Tahiti. Tahiti is both a single island and a group of 118 islands spread out over 2 million square miles (5 million sq km) of the South Pacific Ocean. Many of the islands are crowned

🌐 GEO GEM

What's in a Name?
Australia's name came from the Latin words *australis incognita,* meaning "unknown southern land."

with jagged peaks, while others appear to barely float above the water. Among the more famous islands are Tahiti, Bora Bora, and the Marquesas, or "The Mysterious Islands."

Vanuatu. The Republic of Vanuatu is an archipelago of 83 islands formed by volcanic activity. Several islands still have active volcanoes, which add to the islands' black sand beaches. The islands, which used to be called New Hebrides, are quite mountainous and have a tropical or subtropical climate.

THERE'S NOTHING LIKE AUSTRALIA

"There's nothing like Australia" is a slogan used to promote tourism in Australia, but there is much truth there: Australia is unique among the continents and other island nations.

The **sixth largest country** in the world, the Commonwealth of Australia is located in the Southern Hemisphere and includes the island of **Tasmania** as well as another 12,000 or so smaller islands in the Indian and Pacific oceans. It is an independent Western-style democracy with a diverse population of more than 20 million. One of the world's most urbanized countries, Australia's population prefers the city to the outback—about 70 percent of the population live in the 10 largest cities. Most of the population is concentrated along the eastern seaboard and the southeastern corner of the continent.

Australia has a land area of 2.9 million square miles (7.7 million sq km)—about the size of mainland United States (minus Alaska). By far, the largest part of Australia is the interior outback, which is all arid or semiarid and accounts for about three quarters of the landmass. Australia is the driest inhabited continent, the flattest, and has the least fertile soils. Nonetheless, Australia does have some mountainous areas and plateaus scattered throughout. Mostly, the landscape has been worn down by erosion over millions of years. Some of the outback is part of the world's oldest land surface.

The southeast and southwest corners of the continent have a temperate climate, while the northern part has a tropical climate. The vegetation varies from rainforest to woodland, and from grassland to desert. The grasslands in eastern Australia are used primarily for sheep and cattle ranches.

Australia has some pretty spectacular landscape features, which is one of the reasons why tourism is such a big industry.

The Great Barrier Reef. The world's largest coral reef lies a short distance off the northeast coast and extends for more than 1,250 miles (2,000 km). Coral reefs are building by living creature, and this one is the world's largest. The Great Barrier Reef consists of about 3,000 separate reefs, is home to some 1,500 species of fish, 400 types of coral, 500 species of seaweed, 16 species of sea snake, and 6 species of sea turtle. It is also an important breeding ground for humpback whales.

The Blue Mountains. Located in the southeast, these mountains get their name from the blue haze caused by oil droplets given off by the eucalyptus trees. The wollemi pine found in a remote valley of the mountains is believed to be representative of trees that existed at the time of

 **GEO GEM**

The Land of Counting Sheep
Sheep outnumber people in Australia and New Zealand.

the dinosaurs, making it a species that has been around for 65 million years.

Mount Augustus. The world's largest monocline was formed when an ancient sandstone seabed lifted and folded all the rocks at a single incline (monocline). Over time the surrounding land was eroded away, leaving this rock formation. It looks like a giant rock in an otherwise flat landscape. Mount Augustus has a central ridge that is almost 5 miles (8 km) long. Geologists estimate the age of the rock at about 1,000 million years old.

Uluru. The world's largest monolith—rock—is also called Ayer's Rock. It is a large sandstone formation in the southern part of the Northern Territory in central Australia. Again, the geologic process that formed this rock happened long ago, and the surrounding plains eroded away to expose it. Uluru is sacred to the Aboriginal people of the area. Uluru features many springs, waterholes, rock caves, and ancient paintings and is famous for appearing to change color as the light strikes it at different angles according to the time of the day and year. At sunset Uluru glows red—a remarkable sight to see.

The Wet Tropics of Queensland. On the northeast coast this rainforest wilderness contains an almost complete record of the major stages in the evolution of plant life on Earth. It is the sole habitat for many rare plants and animals and contains the widest range of animal species in Australia.

The Tasmanian Wilderness. Tasmania is an is-

🌐 GEO GEM

Australia's Barring Role
Australia was first settled by Europeans as a penal, or prison, colony.

land off the southern coast of Australia; the wilderness covers about 20 percent of the island. It is one of only three temperate wilderness areas remaining in the Southern Hemisphere and is a major area for plant diversity. Its Huon pines—

GEO GEM

Counting on Coal

Australia is the world's largest net exporter of coal, accounting for 29 percent of global coal exports.

some of them 2,000 years old—are among the most ancient trees in the world. As you'd expect, it is home to the fierce little Tasmanian devil as well as several other animal species that are now extinct on mainland Australia.

Tie Me Kangaroo Down, Sport

Landscape features, such as the ones above, do draw tourists. But the one fact that sticks in every schoolchild's mind is the fact that Australia is home to kangaroos—marsupials that gestate their young in external pouches. In the simplest terms, when Australia broke away from Antarctica about 140 million years ago and drifted north into warm waters (a process that continues to this day), the land became isolated from the other continents, favoring the evolution of these unique mammals. The fact that Australia never experienced an Ice Age, unlike the other continents, means the environment remained relatively stable over 40 million years when other continents went through major periods of animal extinctions. And so Australia is home to the kangaroo, platypus, koala bear, wombat, and kookaburra. In fact, more than 80 percent of the country's flowering plants, mammals, reptiles, and frogs are unique to Australia, along with most of its freshwater fish and almost half of its birds.

Natural Resources

Australia has developed major mining industries around its bauxite, coal, copper, gold, and iron ore. Despite its dry climate, Australia's agriculture is an important segment of the economy, along with established sheep farming and cattle ranching and a growing wine industry. Additionally, Australia's climate and dramatic scenery have made tourism a major industry.

HOME OF THE KIWIS: NEW ZEALAND

New Zealanders are called Kiwis, an affectionate term that refers to the flightless kiwi bird—and not the tasty green fruit with the hairy brown skin that is also known as the Chinese gooseberry.

Lying in the southwest Pacific, south and east of Australia, New Zealand consists of two main islands—the North Island and the South Island—and several smaller islands. The massive Southern Alps form the backbone of the South Island. To the east of the Southern Alps is rolling farmland. Because the South Island is about a third bigger than the North Island, it is sometimes called the Mainland. The North Island of New Zealand has a spine of mountain ranges running through the middle, with gentle rolling farmland on both sides. The central North Island is dominated by a volcanic plateau, an active volcanic and thermal area.

Volcanoes and mountains suggest a lot of action

GEO GEM

Willy-Willies

Tropical Revolving Storms (TRS) are the stuff of legend and the cause of plenty of human misery. These storms are hurricanes in the Caribbean and typhoons in the Indian Ocean. Willy-willies strike in Australia.

THE INTERNATIONAL DATELINE

Exactly halfway around the world from Greenwich, New England, is the International Dateline, an imaginary line that runs through the Pacific and is where the day officially begins, according to the world's clocks. The line would go through the island of Kiribati, had the people been okay with the notion of the country using different calendar dates for the same 24-hour period. So the line is not exactly straight.

caused by the motion of tectonic plates, and this is indeed the case. The North Island and some parts of the South Island sit on the Australian Plate, while the rest of the South Island sits on the Pacific Plate. Because these plates are constantly shifting and grinding into each other, New Zealand gets a lot of earthquake and volcano action.

The rift that separated Australia from New Zealand happened about 100 million years ago, just about the time mammals were emerging. Because of this critical timing, New Zealand had few mammals until humans spread across the globe 80 million years later. There were, however, plenty of flightless—and wingless—birds, including the now-extinct 15-foot moa, which provided food for the first Polynesian Maori settlers who arrived around A.D. 800.

The first European explorer was a Dutchman named Abel Tasman (hence the name, the Tasman Sea, which separates Australia and New Zealand), and he named the land Niuew Zeeland, after the province of Zeeland in the Netherlands.

Later the region was colonized by the British following brutal conflicts among Maori tribes. The Maori stopped fighting each other and focused on fighting the Europeans. In 1840 the Maori signed a treaty that ceded sovereignty to Queen Victoria while retaining territorial rights. Then the British began settling in New Zealand in earnest, triggering a series of land wars that ended with the defeat of the natives. The Maori were given the vote in 1867 and continued to struggle to hold on to their culture and ancestral lands. New Zealand became self-governing in 1856, a dominion in 1907, fully independent in 1947. Today the Maori make up about 14 percent of the population, and their culture is reflected in the prominence of Maori place names, art, and customs.

Spectacular Scenery, Urban Population

Despite, or perhaps because of, New Zealand's spectacular scenery, about 90 percent of the population live in the cities. The scenery includes the vast mountain chain of the Southern Alps (larger than the French, Austrian, and Swiss Alps combined), the volcano region of the North Island, fiords, glaciers, lakes, rainforests, and extensive grassy plains.

New Zealand experiences a temperate climate, with summer from December through February and winter from June through August. Agriculture, horticulture, forestry, fisheries, geothermal energy, and minerals are the primary natural resources of New Zealand. New Zealand exports a lot of lamb, beef, and wool.

WHERE THE U.S. DAY BEGINS

Although the United States is based on the North American continent, the state of Hawaii is technically part of Polynesia. Guam, American Samoa, and the Northern Mariana Islands are territories of the United States, also in the Pacific.

Hawaii. The youngest U.S. state consists of hundreds of volcanic islands spread over 1,500 miles (2,400 km) in Polynesia. The

THE WORLD'S MOST ACTIVE VOLCANO

Mount Ruapehu is one of the world's most active volcanoes and the largest active volcano in New Zealand. It is the highest point in the North Island and includes three major peaks with a deep active crater sitting between the peaks. The volcano began erupting at least 250,000 years ago, and it isn't done yet; there have been major eruptions in 1895, 1945, and 1995, as well as at least 60 minor eruptions since 1945.

Between major eruptions a warm acidic crater lake forms, fed by melting snow. Major eruptions expel the lake water and deposit a dam across the lake's outlet. Eventually, the lake refills and the dam collapses, causing a mudflow known as a **lahar** (originally an Indonesian word). Lahars have the consistency, viscosity, and approximately the same density of concrete: fluid when moving; solid when stopped.

Most recently, Ruapehu erupted in October 2006. The small eruption created a volcanic earthquake of magnitude 2.8, sending a water plume 650 feet (200 m) into the air and 20-foot (6-m) waves crashing into the wall of the crater. It wasn't until March 2007 that the dam holding back the crater lake burst, sending a lahar down the mountain. An estimated 49.5 million cubic feet (1.4 million cu m) of mud, rock, and water thundered down the Whangaehu river. (Other disastrous lahar flows in recent memory include the Nevado del Reiz eruption in Colombia in 1985 and the Mount Pinatubo eruption in the Philippines in 1991.)

A similar situation exists near Mount Rainier in the United States. The U.S. Geological Survey (USGS) has set up lahar warning sirens in Pierce County so that people can flee an approaching mudflow.

archipelago begins in the east with the island of Hawaii and ends almost at the international date line with a small speck in the ocean called Kure Atoll. The eight main islands of Hawaii—Oahu, Hawaii (called the Big Island), Maui, Kauai, Lanai, Molokai, Niihau, and Kahoolawe—contain more than 99 percent of the state's land area and all but a handful of its people. Hawaii has a tropical climate, lush tropical vegetation, beautiful beaches, and volcanic mountains.

Guam. "Where America's Day Begins" is the motto of this organized, unincorporated territory. An island of 209 square miles (541 sq km), Guam is the largest and southernmost of the Mariana Islands. It is located in a region known as "typhoon alley," and it is prone to earthquakes due to its position on the edge of the Pacific Plate near the Philippine Plate. The former Spanish colony was a prize for the United States following the Spanish-American War. Today the government is civilian, and Guam's economy is supported by tourism and the presence of U.S. military personnel. A coral reef with deepwater channels surrounds most of Guam. Sandy beaches, sheer limestone cliffs, and mangroves characterize the coastline. The climate is tropical marine.

Northern Mariana Islands. Part of the same island chain as Guam, the Northern Mariana Islands are under U.S. administration as part of the U.N. Trust Territory

🌐 GEO GEM

Marsupial Mania

More than 120 species of marsupials, mammals that give birth to very immature babies who continue to develop in their mothers' pouches, live in Australia today. These include kangaroos, koalas, Tasmanian devils, wallabies, and wombats.

of the Pacific. The people of the Northern Mariana Islands decided in the 1970s not to seek independence but instead to forge closer links with the United States. A covenant to establish a commonwealth in political union with the United States was approved in 1975. A new government and constitution went into effect in 1978. About 90 percent of the population lives on the island of Saipan.

GEO GEM

Hottest Spot on Earth
The hottest average temperature on Earth is in western Australia, where it averages 96°F (35.5°C) year-round.

American Samoa. American Samoa is an unorganized, unincorporated territory of the United States. It consists of five major volcanic islands and two coral atolls in the heart of Polynesia, 2,500 miles south-southwest of Honolulu and 1,800 miles north-northeast of New Zealand. It is the only U.S. jurisdiction south of the equator.

Chapter 9

Antarctica

The frozen land of snow and rock that forms our southern-most continent is owned by no one, and no country claims it, at least for now. Of all the facts about Antarctica, its unclaimed nature is, perhaps, most unique. Then again, it is the coldest, windiest, driest, loneliest, and least hospitable place on Earth.

A LAND OF ICE AND SNOW

Point by point, Antarctica is the most extreme location on planet Earth.

The Land. Surrounded by the Southern Ocean, Antarctica is an ice-locked landmass located at the South Pole. Including its permanent ice, Antarctica has an area of about 5.5 million square miles (14.3 million sq km), which makes it the **fifth largest continent.** It is the most isolated continent on Earth because it is 600 miles (1,000 km) away from the southern-most tip of South America, its nearest neighbor.

The continent is divided into two regions, **East Antarctica** and **West Antarctica.** East Antarctica, located mainly in the eastern longitudes, is more than three times the size of West Antarctica. Underneath its icecap is geologically old rock, largely above sea level. In contrast, more recent **volcanic action** played a role in forming West Antarctica. Under the weight of its ice, much of the land, which seems to be a group of islands held together by permanent ice, is actually below sea level. Probably the best-known volcano on Antarctica is **Mount Erebus,** which is part of the **Pacific Ring of Fire.** With a summit elevation of 12,448 feet (3,794 m), it looms over McMurdo Station, a U.S. research base on Ross Island.

Mountains and Valleys. The **Transantarctic Mountains** separate the eastern half of the continent from the western half with an S-shaped chain that spans about 3,000 miles (4,800 km). In many places the mountains are mostly buried, but the exposed peaks often have bare jagged-edged faces and reach elevations of more than 14,000 feet (4,270 m). The

EXACTLY WHERE IS THE SOUTH POLE?

If one could insert a rod through the entire planet to show how the Earth rotates, it would go through the North and South poles. In the Arctic the rod would have to be inserted into the seabed of the Arctic Ocean. In Antarctica the South Pole lies inland, and the exploring team of Norwegian polar explorer Roald Amundsen planted the first flag there, followed 33 days later by an ill-fated British-led expedition headed by Robert Falcon Scott. Today the geographic South Pole is the site of the Amundsen-Scott Station, a U.S. scientific base. The pole, meanwhile, is ceremoniously moved every New Year's Day to accommodate the fact that it is on an ice sheet that moves about 33 feet (10 m) every year. But don't confuse the geographic South Pole (0°longitude) with the magnetic south pole. That's about 1,700 miles (2,740 km) away.

highest-known point is in the Ellsworth Mountains, where the bare top of **Vinson Massif** reaches 16,864 feet (5,140 m) above sea level.

In addition to mountains, there are three dry, barren valleys—the Wright, Taylor, and Victoria valleys.

GEO GEM

Adapting to the Cold

The Antarctic cod can survive the cold Southern Ocean because of its ability to lower its freezing point to 28°F (-2°C) and lower its heart rate to six beats per minute.

These valleys, say geologists, haven't seen any rain or snow for thousands of years—some even say at least 1 million! Each valley is about 25 miles (40 km) long and 3 miles (5 km) wide.

Ice Sheet. With the exception of a few bare peaks and "dry" valleys, almost all of this land is covered by an immense ice sheet an average of 1 mile (1.6 km) thick and holding 70 to 90 percent of the Earth's freshwater reserves. Its greatest known thickness is 15,670 feet (4,776 m). In some places the surface of the icecap is fractured by wide cracks, or crevasses, often hidden by thin "bridges" of snow.

Along the coast the ice sometimes forms enormous floating sheets called **ice shelves.** The largest are the Ross Ice Shelf, the Ronne Ice Shelf, the Larsen Ice Shelf, and the Filchner Ice Shelf. Some ice shelves are fed in part by huge freshwater **glaciers** moving down mountain valleys to the coasts. There are also glaciers that flow directly into the sea as long floating tongues; these are called glacier tongues or iceberg tongues. The **Lambert Glacier** on the eastern half of the continent is 25 miles (40 km) wide and more than 248 miles (400 km) long, making it the **largest glacier** on Earth.

Each summer tons of icebergs break off the edges of the ice shelves and float north. Sea ice—frozen seawater that forms during the winter—also breaks up during the summer, giving rise to freely floating ice known as pack ice.

Generally, the icebergs are larger than they appear, since only 10 to 15 percent is visible above the surface of the water. The largest one ever measured was 208 miles (335 km) long by 60 miles (97 km) wide. Scientists estimated that if that one iceberg was melted and the water captured, it would provide enough fresh water to supply London, England, for 700 years.

Elevation. Because the snow never melts, it never goes away—ever. So it builds up, and up. The average elevation of Antarctica is about 7,500 feet (2,286 m), which makes it the **highest continent** on Earth. The high elevation also explains why it is colder at the South Pole than the North Pole. The North Pole is at sea level, and the South Pole is at 9,300 feet (2.900 m); air is cooler at higher elevations.

Climate. Despite all the ice and snow, Antarctica is the **driest continent.** The annual snowfall in the interior of the continent is only 1 to 2 inches (2.5 to 5 cm), although more falls along the coast and on the windward side of coastal mountains—10 to 20 inches (25 to 51 cm) per year.

Because of the way the Earth tilts on its axis as it rotates around the Sun, both polar regions experience one long winter night and one long summer day. The tilt of the Earth also affects

---

🌍 GEO GEM

Neither Rain, Nor Sleet, Nor Gloom of Night

One hundred years after Sir Douglas Mawson was the first Australian to explore Antarctica in 1911, Australia set up a branch of its post office—the first post office on Antarctica—to accommodate the increasing number of scientists and tourists who visit Antarctica each summer.

the angle at which the Sun's radiation hits the Earth. When it is directly overhead at the equator, it strikes the polar regions at more indirect angles. As a result, the Sun's radiation generates much less heat at the poles, even though the polar regions receive as many hours of daylight as the rest of the world.

Temperatures are pretty cold in Antarctica, but the coastal regions

 **GEO GEM**

You Call That Warm?

Although some areas do warm up a bit in the summer, the South Pole, which is located inland on the polar plateau at an altitude of 9,300 feet, does not. The maximum temperature recorded at the South Pole is still well below freezing at 7.5°F (-13.6°C), recorded on December 27, 1978.

are generally warmer than the interior of the continent. The Antarctic Peninsula has even experienced temperatures as balmy as 50°F (10°C) in the summer, but the average summer coastal temperatures are generally around 32°F (0°C). During the dark winter months, temperatures drop drastically; the warmest temperatures range from −4° to −22°F (−20 to −30°C) at the coast. In the colder interior, winter temperatures range from −40° to −94°F (−40 to −70°C).

Winds are constant and fierce, averaging around 50 to 90 miles (80 to 145 km) per hour, but the winds that accompany blizzards are worse, gusting to more than 120 miles (193 km) per hour. They are among the strongest winds on Earth.

A Major Player on Earth's Climate

Antarctica plays a major role in the Earth's climate (as does the Arctic). The icecaps reflect heat from the Sun back into the atmosphere, preventing the Earth from overheating. Also, there is a fairly constant process of massive icebergs breaking away and flowing north to mix with warmer waters from the Atlantic, Pacific, and Indian oceans, producing currents, clouds, and complex weather patterns.

A change in the climate in Antarctica would affect the entire planet. For example, if all of its ice melted, global sea levels would rise by about 200 feet (65 m), flooding the world's major coastal cities and vast areas of low-lying land. Even if only one-tenth of Antarctica's ice were to slide into the sea, sea levels would rise by 20 feet (6 m) and cause significant damage to low-lying coastal areas.

THE DRIFTING CONTINENT

One thing is for sure, Antarctica wasn't always a frozen continent, and the proof is in fossils and seams of coal found in two regions in Antarctica: in the Transantarctic Mountains and Prince Charles Mountains. Coal is formed from the dead remains of trees, ferns, and other plants that lived 300 to 400 million years ago. Coal in Antarctica means that the climate once supported lush vegetation, which means it was warmer and wetter at some point in its history.

Geologists believe that millions of years ago, Antarctica was part of a larger continent called Gondwanaland, which formed from the breakup of Panagea. About 200 million years ago, Gondwanaland broke apart into the separate continents of Antarctica, Africa, Australia, South America, and India. India collided and merged with Asia; Antarctica and the

---

🌍 **GEO GEM**

Well, Blow Me Down!
The highest recorded winds in Antarctica were clocked at Dumont d'Urville station on July 1972. The wind speed hit 199 mph (327km/h).

other continents drifted away from each other. That continental drift continues today.

PENGUINS: THE CONTINENT'S MOST FAMOUS RESIDENTS

Who lives on Antarctica? Mostly research scientist and penguins. However there are numerous species of other mammals, other birds, and fish that also brave the air and waters of the harshest continent.

🌐 GEO GEM

So Near and Yet So Far
South America is the nearest continent to Antarctica—a mere 600 miles (1000 km) away. Unfortunately, the two continents are separated by the Drake Passage—the roughest patch of ocean in the world. Australia is 1,550 miles (2,500 km) away, and South Africa is 2,500 miles (4,000 km) away.

First, the research scientists. Before there were research scientists, there were explorers, lots of them. Speculation over the existence of an "unknown southern land" was not confirmed until the early 1820s when British, American, Norwegian, and Russian whalers and explorers began sailing around the Antarctic Peninsula region and other areas south of the Antarctic Circle. It was probably an American who made the first landing on Antarctica in 1821; Captain John Davis was hunting seal. By 1840 it was pretty much established that Antarctica was indeed a continent and not just a group of islands. Just about everyone wanted a piece of the Antarctica pie. Claims on the territory were made by Argentina, Australia, Brazil, Chile, France, Great Britain, Germany, New Zealand, and Norway. The United States and Russia reserved the right to make claims. Enter the International Council of Scientific Unions, which organized an eighteen-month program of scientific study in Antarctica, from July 1, 1957 until December 31, 1958. The unprecedented

🌍 GEO GEM

A Shifty Pole

The magnetic South Pole shifts about 5 miles (8 km) a year and is now located at about 66°S and 139°E on the Adélie Coast of Antarctica.

cooperation among scientists eventually led to all the parties agreeing to the Antarctic Treaty of 1959.

The Antarctic Treaty was signed by Argentina, Australia, Belgium, Chile, France, Great Britain, Japan, New Zealand, South Africa, the U.S.S.R. and the United States. The two major accomplishments of the treaty were to preserve Antarctica for peaceful purposes and to avoid a confrontation on the issue of territorial claims. Today some 30 countries operate either summer-only or year-round research stations on the land and in the surrounding oceans. The population of scientists and families varies from approximately 4,000 persons during the summer season to 1,000 persons during winter. Additionally Antarctica is beginning to attract tourists who wish to see its pristine environment before it is too altered.

Humans are the largest mammals that live on the land in Antarctica. But the water has a surprising amount of marine life from krill to penguins to seals. A few fish have developed their own form of antifreeze over the centuries to prevent ice crystals from forming in their bodies, while others have evolved into cold-blooded species to survive the cold.

Capturing far more attention than the humans are the six species of penguins that live on Antarctic year round (Adélies, Chinstraps, Emperors, Gentoos, Macaronis, and Rockhoppers). Originally adapted to warmer climates, these "flippered flyers" seemed to have evolved to thrive in a colder climate as the continent began drifting south 40 to 50 million years ago. Their adaptations include oily, unwettable feathers on the outside, covering a layer of soft down that trap body heat. Under the skin is a very efficient insulating layer of blubber. Their bones are not hollow like other birds, and this allows them to dive efficiently in pursuit of food as well as avoid hungry predators, such as seals and killer whales.

Other denizens of the deep south include sea spiders, crab, krill, shrimp, limpets, snails, octopus, sponges, jellyfish, and anemones. The mammal list includes seals, whales, and porpoises. There are about 35 species of seabirds that live south of the Antarctic Convergence, which is where the cold Southern Ocean waters meet the warmer subtropical waters of the Pacific, Atlantic, and Indian oceans. The largest purely terrestrial animal is an insect: The Belgica Antarctica is a tiny, flightless midge.

What Antarctica Is Telling Us about Global Warming

Much of the research that goes on in Antarctica is related to determining if the icecap on Antarctica is changing due to the burning of fossil fuels. Scientists have hypothesized that pollution prevents the heat energy of the earth from escaping into the outer atmosphere, an effect known as "the greenhouse effect." The warming of the planet through this process could cause some or all of the icecap to melt, flooding many cities and lowland areas. Also, because the polar regions are the engines that drive the world's weather system, weather could be affected throughout.

There is a growing body of evidence showing

GEO GEM

More Sun Does Not Equal More Heat

During the summer more solar radiation reaches the South Pole than is received in an equivalent period at the equator.

that the south polar icecap has, in fact, fluctuated dramatically in the past few million years, vanishing completely from the continent once and from its western third several times. These collapses in the ice structure might have been caused by climatic change or by volcanic eruptions under the ice. According to NASA, Antarctica lost about 36 cubic miles (152 cu km) of ice between 2002 and 2005. During that same period, greenhouse gases also rose. Some 98 percent of the world's scientists think that the burning of fossil fuels and other activities of man are causing this measurable warming.

THE HOLE IN THE OZONE LAYER

The ozone layer in the Earth's stratosphere protects life on Earth from absorbing dangerous levels of ultraviolet light. As the spring sun warms the atmosphere over the South Pole, the ozone layer in Earth's stratosphere seasonally thins (often referred to as the "ozone hole"). Since the ozone hole was first observed in 1980, scientists have recorded greater destruction of the layer each year, with the seasonal hole growing and lasting for longer intervals each year. The ozone hole above Antarctica now covers 10.4 million square miles (27 million sq km). Scientists have identified various chemicals created and used by humans, such as chlorofluorocarbons (CFCs), as the cause of this destruction, and bans on uses of these chemicals have begun in some countries.

Does the ozone layer matter? Scientist hypothesize that the increased exposure to ultravio-

🌐 GEO GEM

Spectacular Light Display

The Antarctic sky is sometimes lit by spectacular displays of the *aurora australis,* or the southern lights. (The northern lights are called the *aurora borealis.*)

let radiation caused by the depleted ozone layer increases the risk of skin cancer, cataracts, and a suppressed immune system in humans. It is also expected to cause harm to terrestrial plants, single-cell organisms, and aquatic ecosystems.

 **GEO GEM**

Active Volcanoes

There are at least two active volcanoes in Antarctica—Mount Erebus, which has a permanent molten lava lake, and Mount Melbourne. There may be more buried beneath the ice.

Index

ENJOY THESE OTHER
READER'S DIGEST BESTSELLERS

I Used to Know That

Make learning fun again with these lighthearted pages that are packed with important theories, phrases, and those long-forgotten "rules" you once learned in school.

Caroline Taggart
ISBN 978-0-7621-0995-1

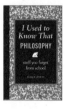

I Used to Know That: Philosophy

Spanning over 2,000 years of philosophical thought, this book covers the main highlights, from Pythagoras to Socrates to Sartre. You'll get an overview of all the major theories, presented in an engaging format.

Lesley Levene
ISBN 978-1-60652-323-0

I Used to Know That: Civil War

Taking you beyond the history book, these pages bring to life colorful personal stories of heroes, brilliant military strategists, blunderers, guerillas, outright villains, spies, secret sympathizers on both sides, and their wives on the home front.

Fred DuBose
ISBN 978-1-60652-244-8

I Used to Know That: Shakespeare

Capturing the unbelievable scope of Shakespeare's influence, this book will surprise and delight you not only with fascinating facts and little-known details of his life but also with the surprising legacy of the language and phrases inherited from his works.

Liz Evers
ISBN 978-1-60652-246-2

i before e (except after c)

Featuring all the memory-jogging tips you'll ever need to know, this fun little book will help you recall hundreds of important facts using simple, easy-to-remember mnemonics from your school days.

Judy Parkinson
ISBN 978-0-7621-0917-3

E=MC²

Anyone frightened by the subject of physics will learn that quantum mechanics doesn't bite—even if it does occasionally bang. Packed with amusing examples, this lively book distills all of the most important discoveries of physics.

Jeff Stewart

ISBN 978–1–60652–167–0

The Classics

From the Acropolis and Homer's *Odyssey* to "carpe diem" and Zeus, this book contains all the stuff you'd ever want to know about classical literature, language, philosophy, art, math, and more—without any of the stuffiness.

Caroline Taggart

ISBN 978-1-60652-132-8

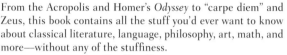

An Apple a Day

Discover the origins and meanings of proverbs—those colorful time-honored truths that enrich our language and culture. You'll learn why these sayings have stood the test of time.

Caroline Taggart

ISBN 978-1-60652-191-5

DON'T FORGET THESE BESTSELLERS

A Certain "Je Ne Sais Quoi"

Easy as Pi

Spilling the Beans on the Cat's Pajamas

Each Book is $14.95 hardcover

For more information visit us at RDTradePublishing.com

E-book editions also available.